TH[E]

MALE FANTASY

Kathleen Turner is chameleon-like. One moment she's a sensual, worldly femme fatale, the dangerous woman who lures men with her beauty and then destroys them with her duplicity; the next, she's a Missouri-born tomboy, the beautiful girl next door.

Tawny-haired, blue-eyed, and throaty-voiced, Kathleen's image was at first pegged by the reviewers as being modeled on the film queens of the 1930s and 1940s. Not so. She grew up abroad and never got the chance to watch old movies. When she sees them now, she says coolly, she feels she's better than those actresses.

Some call her cold, arrogant, and self-centered; others say she's gracious, witty, and professional. Eight movies in six years have poised her on the threshold of superstardom, astonishing critics and captivating fans with her virtuosity, her style, her eroticism, and most of all her range. And she's just getting started!

Kathleen Turner

Rebecca Stefoff

ST. MARTIN'S PRESS/NEW YORK

All insert photographs from Phototeque.

KATHLEEN TURNER

Copyright © 1987 by Rebecca Stefoff

Published by arrangement with the author

ISBN: 0-312-90604-8   Can. ISBN: 0-312-90605-6

Printed in the United States of America

First St. Martin's Press mass market edition/April 1987

10 9 8 7 6 5 4 3 2 1

ACKNOWLEDGMENTS

Special thanks for their assistance go to Geraldine Duclow, head of the Theatre Collection of the Free Library of Philadelphia; Nancy Meyer, of Twentieth Century-Fox in Philadelphia; and Laurie Lennard and Charlene Sullivan, on the staff of NBC-TV's *Late Night with David Letterman*.

Introduction:
The Princess of Paradox

Kathleen Turner is made up of opposites and contradictions. She's the hottest new Hollywood property of the 1980s, one of the most skilled and polished actresses to emerge in years. Yet many of her fans—including some prominent film critics—don't even recognize her when they see her on the street or in a new movie. Some actresses —Joan Collins, Katharine Hepburn, or Sally Field, for example—always play themselves and are instantly recognizable, on screen or in real life. But Kathleen Turner is a chameleon. One moment she's a sensual, worldly femme fatale, the dangerous woman who lures men with her beauty and then destroys them with her duplicity; the next, she's a Missouri-born tomboy, the perfect, traditional girl next door.

In two movies, *Body Heat* and *Crimes of Passion*, she acted in some of the most torrid sex scenes ever to steam off the screen. One male costar described her figure as "a body you shouldn't be allowed to go out in." Another said she had "a behind you'd like to eat lunch off of." Tawny-haired, blue-eyed, and throaty-voiced, she's been called "the ultimate male fantasy," yet she's a conventionally monogamous woman who didn't date much and has spent her share of Saturday nights at home alone. After *Body Heat*, critics and reviewers went wild with comparisons to every screen goddess from Mary Astor to Lauren Bacall. They were certain that Kathleen had modeled her look, her voice, even her hairstyle on the film queens of the 1930s and 1940s. Not so, says Kathleen. She grew up abroad and never watched old movies on late-night television. When she sees them now, she says coolly, she feels she's better than those actresses.

Some of those who have met her or worked with her call her cold, arrogant, and self-centered; others say she's gracious, witty, and professional. She was involved in one of the most bitter and notorious contract disputes in recent film history, a $25,000,000 lawsuit over *The Jewel of the Nile*, yet she denies accusations that she has a bitchy "star" temperament. Eight movies in six years—a short but brilliant career—have poised her on the threshold of superstardom, yet she says she's not interested in the trappings of celebrity. She lives quietly with her husband of two years in New York City, outside the mainstream of the movie world, because Los Angeles has no "depth" and bores her. Early in her career, she created something of a mystique by shunning the limelight and brusquely turning down requests for interviews, but after the success of *Romancing the Stone* she reversed her policy on publicity; she even posed for the cover of *Playboy*.

Movie industry insiders have praised her careful, imaginative choice of roles. In her first movie, she played a seductive, destructive femme fatale. Although her stunning debut was widely acclaimed, she turned down script offers for a year afterward. She found that directors expected her to repeat her *Body Heat* role, and she refused to be typecast as the screen siren of the decade. She gambled with her career, sitting on the sidelines and waitressing to pay the rent, until she had the chance to play exactly the opposite of her *Body Heat* character—a slapstick spoof of a sex goddess in a Steve Martin comedy.

As if to underscore her contrary qualities, she is drawn to roles that force her to reveal more than one side of herself during the course of the movie. One of her most powerful and memorable screen characters is the ultimate split personality: a prude by day and a whore by night. Her best-known and most popular character, Joan Wilder of *Romancing the Stone* and *The Jewel of the Nile*, showed the world the dazzling adventuress hidden in the heart of a not-quite-frumpy spinster.

Kathleen claims that Joan is her own favorite

of all the characters she's played. "She was my first sympathetic character," she says. "I had played two villainesses, women who were virtually hissed off the screen, and after *Romancing the Stone,* people would come up to me and say with surprise, 'You know, you're nice.' I would tell them, 'Yes, I am, thank you.' " Kathleen makes a point of never identifying her characters with her own feelings or experiences, except in one case. She drew upon her single years, living alone with her cat in an apartment on Manhattan's West 57th Street, to create the early Joan, the solitary writer of romance novels before her adventures begin. "I'm more like Joan than any of my other characters," she admits.

This revelation aside, Kathleen Turner rarely talks about her personal life. She prefers to be known for her work and to let that work speak for itself, but it's clear that her chameleonlike talent and her passionate drive for success have roots in her unusual childhood.

1

Not-So-Humble Beginnings

Mary Kathleen Turner was born on June 19, 1954, in Springfield, Missouri. Although her rather straitlaced father and her practical mother would probably have scoffed at an astrological forecast, Kathleen grew up to show the Gemini's typical "split personality": mercurial, charming, stubborn, active, creative, curious, extremely intelligent and enthusiastic, but with a mysterious dark side that can sometimes appear driven, cruel, or selfish. Coincidentally, her first part on Broadway was in Albert Innaurato's hit play *Gemini*.

Her parents had wanted to name her Kathleen Mary Turner. Her initials, however, would have been KMT: the acronym of the Kuomintang, the Chinese Communist Party. For most parents, that wouldn't have been an obvious problem, but Richard Turner and his wife weren't like most parents.

Richard Turner, Kathleen's father, was born

in China, where his grandfather had been a Methodist missionary. He was raised there by his maiden aunts, and Kathleen feels that their old-fashioned Victorian principles had a great influence on her father's personality and, later, on her own family life. She describes him as proud and patriotic. "I don't think he ever lived in the United States for more than a few months," she says, "and yet he was totally American, but brought up with a British education." Just before her father was supposed to leave for college, World War II arrived in the East and the Japanese occupied Shanghai. Richard Turner spent the next four years interned, like many Europeans and Americans, in a Japanese prison.

Kathleen has been told that her six-foot-tall father weighed "something like 120 pounds" when he came out of prison. "He didn't talk about it much," she recalls. "I wish he had." He entered the diplomatic service and was posted in Shanghai, where he met and married Kathleen's mother.

"My mom is a very gutsy woman," Kathleen says proudly. "She grew up in Missouri. She taught school for a year and didn't like it, so right after the war she went into government service and was sent to Shanghai. Just to pack up and leave like she did for China was an amazing thing." Along with many other Westerners, the Turners were thrown out of China in 1949 by the

Communists, thus the decision to ban the initials KMT.

After 1949, the Turners were globe-trotting diplomats, with a new posting to a U.S. consulate every two years or so. Their four children were born within six years in four different countries. The first, Kathleen's sister, was born in Tokyo, Japan. The second, her older brother, in Belgium. Kathleen was the third child and the only one born in the States—in Springfield while her mother was home on leave visiting Kathleen's grandparents. Soon after, the family moved to Canada, where Kathleen spent her early childhood.

She remembers herself as a dramatic, theatrical child, always fantasizing adventures, much like Joan Wilder. "I liked creeping around things," she recalls. "Someone was always after me, I was always in danger from someone." The house she lived in in Canada had a long stairway with a red carpet and a big mirror at the head of the stairs. "I'd crawl up to the top," she says, "and leap out in front of this mirror at the risk of falling backwards down the stairs—just for effect!"

After Canada, the Turners spent several months in Missouri while Kathleen's father studied Spanish in preparation for his next post: Cuba. Kathleen had attended nursery school in Canada, where the boys and girls started every day by singing the British national anthem, "God Save the Queen." Her parents decided to enroll her in nursery school in Missouri. "I was very frightened, but I was willing," she says. "The teacher started to play the piano, and I blasted out 'God Save the Queen' while everybody else was singing, 'My country, 'tis of thee.' "

Kathleen was in kindergarten in Cuba when the Communists, under Fidel Castro, took over the government in 1959. She went to a Cuban school, and she remembers that the teachers were among Castro's earliest supporters. One day, her teacher told the class to close their eyes and pray to God for candy. When they opened their eyes, there was no candy, of course. Then the teacher told them to close their eyes and pray to Castro for candy. While they prayed, she put candy on each desk. When the children opened their eyes, the teacher asked them, "Who loves you, God or Castro?"

Because the United States did not immediately break off relations with Cuba, the Turners didn't leave the country at once. But their final days in Cuba were filled with fear, as the pro-Castro faction was hostile to Americans. "I remember our dogs being poisoned and tarantulas being left in the house and our maid being afraid to work for us," Kathleen says. She also recalls a taped message that was placed on all the telephone lines: it repeated "Castro is our salvation" over and over. One day, Kathleen's gutsy mother lost patience and screamed into the phone, "Castro is an asshole!"

In what must have seemed to her parents to be a terrifying and frustrating repetition of their expulsion from Shanghai, the Turners hastily left Cuba in 1960. Their next stop was Caracas, the capital of Venezuela. Kathleen attended junior high school, learned fluent Spanish, and sang in the English choir. She was lively and active—"a real tomboy, my mother could hardly get me into a dress," she says. And she loved school plays and the productions of the community theater. At that time, though, she had no desire to act. Instead, she wanted to dance. She was taken by her mother to the ballet during a family visit to Washington, D.C., which she left thinking, "I want to be a ballerina." It wasn't until the Turners moved to London, where Dick Turner was to be U.S. consul, that Kathleen discovered her passion for acting.

On their first night in London, Kathleen's parents took her to see Angela Lansbury in *Mame.* "We had tickets in the fourth tier of one of those old theaters, where you're afraid to take a step, way the hell up there," she says. "I remember being swept away, thinking, 'Gee, this is what I'm going to do to earn a living,' which is different from just deciding to act." After that night, she went to the theater twice a week to revel in performances by Christopher Plummer, Diana Rigg, Paul Scofield, and others. She also made pilgrimages to the annual Shakespeare Festival at the playwright's home, Stratford-on-Avon.

Her father didn't approve of her decision to make a career in acting, Kathleen says, "because it had never been part of our world; it was unthinkable. I think he thought I'd grow up and marry well, be a terrific diplomatic wife." Despite his misgivings, however, he allowed her to enroll in London's Central School of Speech and Drama while she also took regular high-school classes.

Kathleen fell in love with London. "I'd make it my home," she now says, "but the tax laws are so cruel." She remembers her high-school years there, from 1969 through 1972, as the best part of her wandering adolescence. She had been living in South America, where a young woman couldn't go anywhere alone ("particularly a blonde *gringa,*" she says), and she loved the sudden new freedom England gave her. "I just jumped on the subway with my brother and rode it all day, not knowing where we were going, just knowing that we were moving and safe, which was wonderful," she recalls. All of Europe was open to her; she could take a ferry to Amsterdam for the weekend whenever she wanted. But although Amsterdam was the drug capital of Europe during the hippie era, Kathleen was a very straight teenager.

"My father was very strict: home by eleven," she says. "There was some dating, but it was very strictly controlled. Premarital sex was unthinkable! I can't believe we were so incredibly naive. There were drugs going on in high school in London—kids were smoking opium—but I never tried anything. I was so brainwashed about being the 'proper person.' " Her father was strict in other ways, too, "very Victorian," as Kathleen says. He disapproved of television, and the children didn't have a lot of exposure to movies and music. The other three were straight-A students, and Kathleen developed a habit of voracious reading that continues today.

She was much more emotional and expressive than her father, which sometimes made communication difficult. "He wasn't very demonstrative with his feelings—he was kind of inhibited that way—and I remember one time I just sat on his lap and said I wouldn't leave until he hugged me. He just thought it was my silliness." Kathleen's need for affection from her father, like her need to perform, may have been the result of sibling rivalry, unavoidable among four children so close in age.

Her older brother remembers Kathleen as "an insanely jealous teenager," and she admits that relationships within the family were sometimes "intense," although they were also warm and loving. The children weren't allowed to fight, but Kathleen fought with her father. During the American bombing of Cambodia, the young Turners joined in the British protest marches. She had to agree not to march on the U.S. embassy, though; her father was afraid the ambassador would look out and say, "Hey, isn't that *Dick Turner's* kid out there?"

The good times in London came to a sad and shocking end in Kathleen's senior year of high school, a week before she graduated. Dick Turner died suddenly. "He had very high blood pressure and something burst and he literally fell down dead," says Kathleen. "It was a very difficult time for all of us." Deeply saddened by her father's death, Kathleen regrets today that he didn't take her seriously as an actor. She says, "It's painful for me not to be able to show him what I've accomplished, that it wasn't just a pipe dream. . . ."

Overnight the young drama student found herself adrift. Her older brother and her sister returned to the States for college; her mother planned to return to her family home in Missouri, taking her younger son with her. But Kathleen's hopes and plans were shattered. "I wanted to study acting," she says, "but I didn't know where to do it if I had to leave England. When my father was alive, I always had the feeling that I could be anywhere in the world and if I could just get to a phone and call Consul Turner I'd be taken care of. His death added to the confusion of not knowing what I was doing." Unable to complete her program at the Central School of Speech and Drama, Kathleen had no choice but to come back to Missouri with her mother.

By the age of eighteen, Kathleen had lived in five countries in both hemispheres. Although her brothers and sister sometimes felt that their cosmopolitan, always-on-the-move existence was a source of destructive pressure, Kathleen viewed it as a delightful adventure. In a way, travel was her first taste of acting. It gave her the opportunity to remake herself at each new destination, to show a new face to the world. As she stood at the rail of the ship carrying her away from Caracas, she thought, "Now I can be *anybody*, because where I'm going, nobody has any idea of who I was before, so I can have a new name, a new personality. . . ." She says today, "The parts of myself I didn't like in Caracas, I didn't have to be in London." During her first month in London, in fact, people called her Doris. She had perky little bangs, like Doris Day, and she acted that character until she "couldn't stand it anymore."

Her flexible lifestyle was a good training ground for her future as a performer. "When you go into a new country and a new school all the time," she says, "there's always a testing period. I never felt I could just walk in expecting to be guided and helped; I had to walk in as if I knew what I were doing. It teaches you how to assume a certain confidence, how to present a certain face. I think that had a lot to do with acting." In all her travels, however, Kathleen had never faced an adjustment as difficult as that which awaited her now that she was returning "home" for the first time since early childhood.

She speaks with admiration of her mother's courage and resourcefulness in the painful time after her father's death: "She went right back to work—just picked up her skills after twenty years of not working and got herself a job as a legal secretary." Things didn't go as smoothly for Kathleen.

"It was probably the worst culture shock I had ever gone through," she recalls. "I showed up in Missouri with a heavy English accent. In my absolute terror, I was determined not to lose this sort of distinction, which I thought of as a great affectation, and the kids were not very understanding or forgiving. They thought I was unbearable."

There was never any doubt that the next step for Kathleen would be college. Education was highly prized in the Turner clan, and all three of Kathleen's siblings were excellent students. "There are a lot of Dr. Turners running around out there," she says proudly. Her sister has a doctoral degree in urban sociology, her older brother in psychology, and her younger brother in political economics. She adds wryly, "I am definitely not the typical member of this family. But who knows? If I'm a star long enough, maybe some college will give me an honorary doctorate!"

Such possibilities were far in the future in 1973, when Kathleen enrolled in the theater program of Southwest Missouri State College in Springfield. The first drawback of American college life was the dorm, where all the single women were supposed to live. "I just hated it," Kathleen says vehemently. "I hated living with a bunch of women, especially ones who talked singsong all the time." She imitates a typical Southern-belle squeal and adds, "They were driving me out of my mind!" One incident in particular illustrates everything she detested about the dormitory mentality. The girls had the habit of putting daily Bible quotes or advertising slogans on the bulletin board; Kathleen remembers that "Today is the first day of the rest of your life" was popular. One day she posted " 'Tis better to reign in Hell than serve in Heaven.—Milton." Later she walked in on a full-blown floor meeting called to discuss her "blasphemous" message. She was told (in a Southern accent), "We respect your freedom under the First Amendment to express yourself as an American citizen, but either you must erase this message or you should really consider moving." Kathleen wangled a note from a psychiatrist to the effect that dorm life was bad for her mental health and moved into an off-campus apartment with a roommate.

Kathleen formed some close friendships in the theater department, but her relations with many of her peers remained strained. "I still came on very British, you know, 'Hello, my name is Kathleen Turn-uh, I'm studying theat-uh,'" she admits. "I got all the Shakespeare parts. I must have really been the pits." She appeared in many productions, was well thought of by her teachers, and was active in the department's summer program, the Tent Theater.

One young New York actress who attended SMSC several years behind Kathleen remembers her well, especially her determination to excel. "I saw her in *Oh, Dad, Poor Dad,*" she says. "Even then, she carried herself like she does now. *She* was sure she'd make it. I guess a belief in your own superiority can carry you over a lot of rough times. I didn't know what had become of her until a few years later. I was in a theater and I saw a preview of *Body Heat.* The camera panned up her leg and when it reached her face I stood up and yelled, 'I know *her!*'"

Three years at SMSC were enough for Kathleen. "I wanted to get into experimental theater, and I couldn't do it there. There was nothing happening," she explains. She bought an old

1965 Oldsmobile 88 for $300, packed her things, and took off for Baltimore, where she finished college at the University of Maryland and earned a Bachelor of Fine Arts degree. It was important to her mother, although Kathleen knew a degree wouldn't do much for her career.

While in Baltimore, she helped found the experimental New Theater. She also auditioned for the prestigious Arena Stage in Washington, D.C. She didn't get a part at the Arena (that came later), but the casting director did give her the name and number of an agent in New York City. Kathleen decided it was time to move again.

She had a good friend who was living in New York, so at least she knew she'd have a place to stay. She loaded a van with her clothes and books —"I didn't have much," she recalls—and headed north, scared and excited. "I was twenty-two, moving to the most exciting city in the world with $100 in my pocket. That was it!" she says. "Nobody told me it was hard to get a job, so I walked into a temporary employment agency and by the third day I was working and I knew I could pay the rent. It was terrific." Kathleen had always liked to feel special and set apart, and being an impoverished waitress in the Big Apple didn't change that: "A friend told me to give myself something special every week so I wouldn't feel like the other millions of people walking around —a cab ride, a bottle of wine, whatever it is,

whether or not you can afford it. Great advice."
She adds, "I also got an agent the first month."

The agent was David Guc of Bloom Associates, who had been recommended to Kathleen by
the casting director of the Arena. The same director had called David to tell him that Kathleen
would be perfect for commercials, so he agreed
to see her. Meeting him in May of 1977 was a
professional and romantic turning point for
Kathleen.

"When she came in she was . . . unfinished
is the best word," Guc recalls. "It was a hot day,
a very hot day. We were both sweaty and unattractive. The first and only thing I paid attention
to was her potential for TV commercials. Her
voice was very strange—deep, with an accent
somewhere between Taiwan and Bolivia."

Her voice, indeed, has become one of Kathleen's most potent and distinctive qualities. It
wasn't always that way. She worked long and hard
to achieve clear diction and the low, vibrant purr
that one critic described as "an amalgam of
honey and sandpaper" (her cigarette habit may
have helped with the huskiness). Tricks imparted
by British drama coaches, such as practicing
speaking with pencil erasers clenched between
the back teeth, gave her control and resonance.
The image she most hates—and one she feels is
common in America—is the beautiful, sexy, expensively dressed woman who makes a grand en-

trance and then ruins the effect by speaking in a whiny, nasal, or screechy voice.

Her voice didn't impress Guc. Neither did anything else about her. Nonetheless, he called in his boss, Michael Bloom, who insisted that Kathleen audition. Her audition was "one of the four best of my career," says Guc. He and Bloom tried to sign this sensational discovery up that very day, but she said she had to take the contract to her lawyer. Her caution was unnecessary. "It was the standard Equity SAG–AFTRA contract," she laughs, "and the lawyer said, 'What do you need me for, honey?'"

Kathleen's career has proved over and over again that casting directors *can* make mistakes. Despite the recommendation from the Arena Stage, she was disastrous in commercials. At twenty-two, she was too young to play a glamorous older woman convincingly, but her voice torpedoed her for young ingenue housewife bits. She remembers one ill-fated audition for a floor-cleaning product: "The copy said, 'Your floor looks so *clean . . .*' I tried ten, fifteen different ways, saying, 'Give me just one more take, one more,' and they were shaking their heads, saying, 'Just believe us.'" Ironically, it was her throaty, purring voice that finally made a truly successful commercial: sales of Van Heusen shirts soared in Canada after she recorded a radio ad for them there.

She didn't score with commercials, but she
stuck with Guc. The two fell in love, and eventually moved in together. It was Kathleen's first
serious romantic involvement, and it lasted for
almost five years. When she speaks of the affair
today, however, she doesn't reveal its emotional
impact, if any. She talks only about how the relationship helped her career: "It was a fabulous
base for me. I was with somebody who was completely involved with my work, what I was trying
to do; everything was feeding into that. It was
incredibly reassuring." She credits Guc, who is
still her agent, with giving her lots of good advice
about her acting as well as negotiating her stage
and screen deals.

Kathleen did a little work in off-off-Broadway shows. Then, only eight months after she had
arrived in New York, she landed the part of Nola
Dancy Aldrich on NBC's soap opera *The Doctors,*
a melodrama centered around the fictitious Hope
Memorial Hospital. By the time Kathleen took
over the part (which had been created by Kathryn
Harrold), the show had been on the air for fifteen
years and had many die-hard fans. They loved
her portrayal of Nola, a bad girl from the wrong
side of the tracks who marries into the town's
richest and most prominent family.

"I had a lot of fun doing Nola and I learned
a lot," Kathleen says. "It was my first camera
work." Nola was a beautiful manipulator, some-

thing like the character of Matty Walker, whom Kathleen would play in *Body Heat*. "But," laughs Kathleen, "even though she thought she was really being nasty, she was actually kind of stupid. She was so transparent that you could see right through her, which was funny."

Kathleen has plenty of praise for her fellow actors on the soap. She feels that there was a lot of talent on the show, but that the scripts were "really dumb." There was no continuity of character, she points out, because new and different writers were constantly coming in at a moment's notice and writing scripts with no reference to the character's past. She gives an example: "One day's script might have a character saying, 'I'm going to try to, uh, fool Jason, so that he doesn't find out I'm, uh, sleeping with this other guy.' The next day, the same character is supposed to say, 'What a delicious irony, my dear! Chronology has nothing to do with it.'"

Nola had a couple of surprises in store for Kathleen. First of all, she had a drinking problem, so Kathleen got very good at acting drunk. ("I never *drank* while I was performing," she jokingly assured David Letterman on his late-night talk show. "I'm not a method actress.") Then, six months into the show, she learned that Nola had a frustrated longing to be a night-club singer. When she said to the producers, "You didn't ask me if I can sing when I auditioned," she was told,

"That's okay—you don't have to be *good*." So Nola developed the habit of singing only when she was drunk. As Kathleen explains it, she'd have a few drinks, climb up on a table, start singing, and then fall off before everyone could hear how bad she was.

Nola also got pregnant during Kathleen's stint on *The Doctors*. "I gave birth after five months, which is some kind of feat," Kathleen says. "They give you these pads to wear, and they gradually get bigger and bigger. I took it all very seriously, studied Lamaze natural-childbirth breathing techniques and everything. Well, the way they stretch everything out on these shows, I was in labor for five days! The funniest thing was as I was lying there supposed to be giving birth, strapped to this table, with glycerin all over my face to look like sweat, the director came out and said, 'That's very good, dear, I can really see what you're going through, but could you try to do it a little more *attractively*?' He had the nurse putting lipstick on me!"

Perhaps the most valuable lesson Kathleen learned from *The Doctors*—even more valuable than the tips on natural childbirth—was the need for artistic control, for an emotional distance between herself and her character. It was a painful lesson to learn. The character of her mother on the show was dying. "For some reason I flashed really badly on Daddy's death," she recollects.

"In the dress rehearsal, I just knew I was going to burst into tears. I thought, 'Okay, just hold it until they tape it. If you are going to go through this, at least use it.' And for the taping, I finally let it go. I was *sobbing*. We finished the show, and I thought it was the most real thing I had ever done. But I saw the show, and it was the worst piece of ham acting I'd ever seen in my life. It just looked absurd." Kathleen now believes that she is most effective as an actor when she shows the audience through disciplined skill what her character is feeling, not when she tries to feel it herself. As a performer, she sees herself as an extra step between the character and the audience. "The audience doesn't really want to step into your life," she states. "They don't want to go through your pain. They want to be touched by it."

While working on the soap, Kathleen also appeared as a featured player on Broadway in *Gemini*, the hit comedy by Albert Innaurato. On August 14, 1978, she replaced Carol Potter in the role of Judith Hastings, an ultra-preppy, rich Radcliffe girl who gets involved with a chubby, introverted boy from South Philadelphia. By that time, the play had been performed more than 500 times. She stayed with the show for nine months, and her schedule was grueling: arriving at NBC studios at seven in the morning and leaving at five in the afternoon, then dashing to the theater, which she would leave at eleven. Not to mention the mental discipline required to create two characters as wildly different as Nola and Judith every day.

The Doctors was good to Kathleen, but after a year and a half she wanted out. She was bored, and she felt she was ready for a bigger, more ambitious project. The producers released her, and her departure was mourned by the fans who had loved to hiss at her drunken villainies. She returned to the stage, appearing in *Travesties* and *The Seagull* at the Manitoba Theatre Center in Winnipeg, Canada, but she grew frustrated with regional theater because, as she says, "there's no money." She decided she was ready to try for a film role.

Guc heard about a part he thought she'd be perfect for in an upcoming movie called *Body Heat.* He called the casting director three times a day, hoping to get an audition for Kathleen. He was turned down every time. Finally he gave up and sent her to Los Angeles to try for another part: a female wrestler in *All the Marbles.*

2

TURNING UP THE HEAT

"Thank God I didn't get that part!" Kathleen now says. The part she didn't get was one of the two women wrestlers managed by Peter Falk in the forgettable comedy *All the Marbles*. At five feet eight inches tall and not too many more than 100 pounds, Kathleen was too tall and slender to make it as a bosomy, muscular wrestler. But she's justifiably thankful that she lost the part. Not only did the film die at the box office, but missing it left her free for one of the most stunning screen debuts in movie history. She didn't luck into her big chance, though; she had to fight for it.

In Los Angeles, Kathleen met Wally Nicita, who just happened to be the West Coast casting director for *Body Heat*, a twisted, sensual tale of lust, murder, and betrayal. She immediately saw Kathleen's potential for the starring role of Matty Walker, the beautiful femme fatale of *Body Heat*, and said, "You have to meet Larry and Fred" (Lawrence Kasdan, writer and director, and Fred

T. Gallo, producer). After a flurry of confusing
telephone calls between the two coasts (the New
York casting director kept saying that Kathleen
had already been tested; she insisted that she
hadn't), Nicita was able to arrange a meeting.
Kathleen showed up "dressed to the nines," as
she describes it, in her highest heels, a slit skirt,
and "all the makeup I could muster," and read
two scenes from the script for Kasdan and Gallo.
She says, "I picked up the script and thought, 'I
know this woman.' That doesn't happen very
often to me. But I knew the rhythms, I knew her
thoughts."

She desperately wanted the part; Kasdan and
Gallo seemed interested, but noncommittal.
After the audition, she was shaking with nervous-
ness as she drove along the Ventura Freeway to
where she was staying. Her unfamiliarity with
California didn't help. "I kept getting lost on this
goddamned freeway," she recalls. "But when I
got home, there was a message on my service to
see them again the next morning. And I thought,
'That can't be all bad.'" At that point, she began
praying she'd be rejected for the Peter Falk film.

When she reported to his office the next day,
Kasdan told her to lie down on a couch—the
casting couch of countless Hollywood jokes, although perfectly innocent in this case. He
handed her a script and asked her to read a scene
that he hadn't yet shown to any of the actresses

who had tried for the part during the previous four months of casting. "I know you haven't seen this," he said, "but try it anyway." It was a demanding scene, central to a believable interpretation of the character. It was the scene where Matty lets slip a few intimate details about her sordid past as a junkie in Chicago—the details that later provide a clue to her identity and motivations. When Kathleen had finished, there was complete silence in the room. Her nerves were at the breaking point, and then Kasdan quietly said, "I never thought I'd hear that scene read exactly as I heard it in my head when I wrote it." Says Kathleen, "It was so wonderfully exciting that we just started laughing."

She still didn't have the part, however. Kasdan and Gallo asked her to test with William Hurt, the outstanding young actor who had proved himself at New York's Circle Repertory and in *Altered States*, with Blair Brown, and *Eyewitness*, with Sigourney Weaver. He had been cast as Ned Racine, Matty's lover. Physical compatibility and on-screen chemistry between the film's two stars were absolutely vital to its success. As moviegoers were to discover, Matty and Ned seem to spend half the movie alone together with their clothes off.

Kathleen and Hurt had met in New York, but they had never worked together, although she had seen him in *Fifth of July* at the Circle. They knew each other only slightly. He arrived in Los Angeles the night before their screen test. They had dinner together to discuss the scenes they'd be doing and to go over the lines. "The first thing he asked me when he picked me up for dinner was, 'How long have you been in L.A.?' " says Kathleen. "I said, 'About ten days,' and he said, 'Thank God!' " It appears Hurt agreed with Kathleen (who calls herself "a snobbish New York actor") that the typical Californian is nothing much to get excited about.

Happily, the two clicked on screen, and that hurdle was past. Even with Kasdan behind her, though, Kathleen was still encountering resistance from executives of the Ladd Company, which was backing the film. They had hoped for the drawing power of a big-name star, and Kathleen was a nobody in Hollywood terms. In addition, they expressed doubts about her versatility: even if she looked good in the intense dramatic moments, could a relatively untested young performer also carry off the lighter scenes that open the movie? The executives demanded a meeting. Kathleen knew it was really a test, a test that would make or break her chance to do the film, once and for all. The outcome of that meeting became something of a minor legend in filmland.

Kathleen tells the story: "The meeting took place in a huge executive office that was all white —white chairs, white couches, white rug, every-

thing white except a big ashtray filled with cigarette butts and ashes. You got the feeling that
they'd been sitting there all day, smoking and
talking about 'the girl.' I had a script in my hand.
One of the vice presidents asked me what I did on
the soap. I said, 'Oh, I got to play drunk a lot.' He
said, 'Okay, do drunk.' So I started acting drunk
and I threw the script onto the table and it hit the
ashtray, and the ashtray just skidded across the
table and onto the floor, scattering ashes and
butts all over the white carpet. I got down on my
hands and knees to pick them up, thinking, 'This
is the most embarrassing moment of my entire
life,' and then I realized they were all *laughing*.
I'm sure that's how I got the part.''

Kathleen wasn't the only risk the studio took
with an unknown quantity. *Body Heat* was also
thirty-two-year-old Kasdan's directorial debut.
He had started out in the industry as a writer.
With only one marketable screenplay to his credit
—*Continental Divide,* which was filmed with John
Belushi and Blair Brown but was not received
with great enthusiasm by either critics or audiences—he was selected by Steven Spielberg and
George Lucas to write the screenplay for a film
that became one of Hollywood's biggest hits
ever: *Raiders of the Lost Ark.* Before Lucas had even
read the script for *Raiders,* he asked Kasdan to
write *The Empire Strikes Back.* After several years of
working on wide-screen adventures, Kasdan

wrote *Body Heat* as an example of the more personal, intimate adult stories he preferred (although he went on to write *Return of the Jedi* at Lucas's request). He intended from the start to direct *Body Heat*. But what might have been disaster—the combination of a neophyte director and an inexperienced actress—turned out to be a triumph for both of them. "I have a lot of chutzpah," Kathleen says with a laugh, "and Larry has an extraordinary grasp of things. I think the fact that he was new to directing worked for me. He was having conferences, taking the time he needed to understand how and why things were being done. That gave me time to listen in and say, 'How are we doing this?' or 'Why is it this way?' A seasoned director would assume I knew everything."

Body Heat, says Kasdan, is essentially the story of people who are "searching around for a quick score, a way to get to it without any pain." The score can be love and sex or money—in the movie it's both, and the two become intertwined until they seem inseparably confused. Ned Racine starts out hoping for nothing more than a roll in the hay with Matty, but eventually he wants not just her, but everything else that her rich, older husband owns. Kathleen says that Kasdan met a woman at a party and was later told that she had married for money alone. His thoughts about the kind of person she might be developed into the character of Matty Walker, the seductive beauty who seems to be the object of Ned's passionate obsession but in reality is the puppetmaster pulling his strings. She plants the notion of her husband's death in Ned's mind, eggs him on to murder and lets him believe it's his idea, professes undying love, and then disappears with the money, leaving Ned to face prison not just for Edmund's murder but also for what looks like her own.

If the story sounds familiar, it is. Kasdan set his story in a melodramatic context shaped by the tradition of *film noir,* dark suspense thrillers of the 1930s and 1940s like *The Big Sleep, Out of the Past, Laura,* and *The Postman Always Rings Twice.* These films have an affinity with—some of them are based on—the writing of Raymond Chandler and James M. Cain. They are glimpses of a world in which nothing is what it seems to be, no motives are ever pure or actions simple, and no one is smart enough or brave enough to escape a twisted and ironic fate.

Body Heat is almost a remake of a 1946 classic based on a novel by Cain: *Double Indemnity,* in which a fatally seductive Barbara Stanwyck cons Fred MacMurray, an insurance salesman who's not as smart as he thinks he is, into killing her husband. The parallels are unmistakable: not just in plot and character but in subplot (the friendly investigator who reluctantly traps the killer, played by Edward G. Robinson in *Double Indemnity* and Ted Danson and J. A. Preston together in *Body Heat*) and dialogue (the teasing double entendres in which Matty and Ned test each other's availability, the "traffic cop" conversation between Stanwyck and MacMurray).

Growing up abroad, Kathleen didn't share the typical American exposure to old movies on late-night television. She claims that she had never seen *Double Indemnity*—either the original movie version or the TV movie with Richard Crenna in the Fred MacMurray role (ironically, Crenna played Edmund Walker, Matty's rich but expendable husband, in *Body Heat*). Although many critics assumed that she had studied Stanwyck's performance, she simply followed Kasdan's direction. She deplored Matty's actions, but she admits that the strength and power of the character appealed to her. "Matty was powerful and deceitful and interesting and attractive," she says. "She was definitely in control of the situation, at whatever the cost. I don't think I'd read a role like that for a woman in film for a long time." Kathleen also developed a sense of what Matty's life before the movie might have been like. "I saw her as having a faded-beauty mother and a rather ineffectual father," she explains. "All her teenage years were spent listening to her mother saying, 'Don't make the same mistake I did. You're too beautiful, you're too smart. Don't settle like I did.' "

Although Kathleen may not have been familiar with classic *film noir*, Kasdan showed that he knew and loved it. Everything about *Body Heat* pays homage to the great movies of the genre. The setting, clothing, and cinematography combine to blur the distinction between past and present. The audience knows it's 1981, yet everything echoes the cinematic past. A band that might have been led by Tommy Dorsey or Glenn Miller plays "That Old Feeling" as Matty makes her first appearance, walking slowly toward Ned in a white sheath dress slit up the thigh. Throughout the movie, she wears updated versions of vintage styles: subtle shoulder pads, short-sleeved fitted blouses, tight skirts. Her only gift to Ned is a hat, a gray fedora that Phillip Marlowe would have recognized instantly. Kasdan had originally planned to shoot the film in New Jersey, but an actors' strike delayed production, so he relocated to Florida, which happens to be the story's setting. It may have been a lucky move; as in the Humphrey Bogart classic *Key Largo*, the oppressive tropical atmosphere is the film's third main character, and faking it in Jersey might not have been as effective as the torrid reality. Everyone in the film sweats constantly. Fans are omnipresent, as though air conditioners hadn't been invented. Swirling nighttime fog, light creeping through

Venetian blinds, a man dressed as a clown who drives past in a forty-year-old red convertible just as Ned is parking his red Corvette—all these 1940s-style images create an uneasy, almost hallucinatory, suspense. John Barry's original music uses a single compelling theme to convey languorous lust at the beginning of the movie and violent tension at its end.

Part of the movie's impact came from the hundreds of tiny touches that foreshadowed the surprise-within-a-surprise climax. Even the opening credits, showing two bodies hazily entwined while a building burns in the background and finally explodes, are like a miniature preview of the story to come: the consuming lust, the fire that doesn't quite destroy Edmund's body, the explosion that finally destroys Ned's belief in Matty. The credit sequence ends with the wail of a police siren, prefiguring poor Ned's fate. The hallway floor where Ned first makes violent love to Matty is the exact place he bludgeons Edmund to death some weeks later. Afterward, although she swears to Ned that she loves him, Matty continues to wear the huge diamond engagement ring Edmund had given her; its cold, baleful glitter flashes disquietingly as she wraps her arms around Ned's neck.

Kathleen says that one of the biggest challenges she faced in creating the character of Matty was to plant enough tiny hints of the truth about her motives. She wanted the audience to be conned along into believing in Matty, just like Ned, but they should later be able to look back on all of her actions and words in light of her betrayal. What seems to be lighthearted badinage is, in retrospect, a chilling announcement of her intentions. At their first meeting, she smiles and says to Ned, "You're not too smart, are you? I like that in a man." Cocky and confident, he thinks she's flirting. As it turns out, she was only telling the bitter truth.

Response to the movie's *film noir* echoes was, for the most part, positive. Most critics recognized Kasdan's work as an admiring tribute to earlier films and had strong praise for his first directorial effort. A few, however, felt that *Body Heat* was just an old story recycled. Pauline Kael, in the *New Yorker*, panned it as derivative and singled out Kathleen's performance as wooden and labored. Another critic complained that the absence of air conditioners made the movie too implausible.

But these negative reactions were lost in the flood of praise that flowed forth from the pens and typewriters of critics and reviewers all over the country. And Kathleen, as an actor new to virtually all of them, received a big share of their attention. Perhaps because the movie so clearly echoed past screen classics, most reviewers compared Kathleen to past screen queens, especially those who had played femme fatale roles. Suddenly, she was the new Ice Princess, Bitch Goddess, temptress, siren—every male fantasy of the beautiful but deadly female. She was identified with Veronica Lake, Mary Astor (who had played opposite Humphrey Bogart in *The Maltese Falcon*), Stanwyck, Lauren Bacall, Lana Turner, Rita Hayworth, Susan Hayward, and others. One reviewer wrote that she had Hayworth's hips, Hayward's voice, and Bacall's hair. Another disagreed, saying it was Lake's hair and Bacall's cheekbones. Still another claimed it was Bacall's voice and Stanwyck's figure!

How did Kathleen react to all these comparisons? Well, partly because she's cool and somewhat sardonic by nature, and partly because she hadn't even seen most of these women on the screen, she didn't get too carried away by it. Preferring to be evaluated on her own merits, she assumed that earlier stars might resent being imitated. " 'The new Lauren Bacall,' " she scoffed. "I kept wondering what *she* would feel like. My God! 'Have you heard about the new *you*?' How rude!" She was delighted, however, with one response to the movie: a note from Barbara Stanwyck. "The only one who could have done it better," Stanwyck wrote, "is me." Kathleen did finally see *Double Indemnity*, several years after *Body Heat* was released.

Kasdan, too, shrugged off the comparisons.

"Kathleen doesn't fit into a niche with anybody," he said. He claims to have selected her for the role because of her striking originality and her "absolutely magnificent vocal quality." The voice, of course, is what prompted many of the comparisons. Kathleen feels that actors today have anonymous voices. Because she has taken the trouble to train hers to project certain qualities, it is reminiscent of the days when actors and actresses had distinctive, memorable voices. She also admits to other similarities between herself and earlier actresses.

"One of the reasons that I'm labeled as being like an old-fashioned female star is that those women were somewhat domineering and intellectually aware, as I have been in some of my roles," she now says. "But when I see those old movies, I think I'm better than some of those actresses." She goes on to explain that, while she may sound arrogant, she means only that she feels she has more freedom to be professional, to accept a variety of challenging roles rather than to develop one screen personality and portray it in every film, as stars of the 1930s and 1940s were expected to do. Whom does she admire among the stars of yesteryear? Stanwyck? Bacall? No, indeed. "Carole Lombard, because she was able to combine being sexy and being funny."

The *film noir* angle wasn't the only thing to attract attention from critics and audiences. *Body*

Heat differed from its predecessors in one important respect: its explicit sexuality (it was rated R), which captured headlines. Even among contemporary films, it was regarded as one of the most sexually direct movies to be made in America in years. Matty and Ned are shown nude and making love in numerous positions and locations: the bed she shares with Edmund, the boathouse, the gazebo (where Matty drops to her knees in front of Ned and the audience hears the sound of a zipper).

Perhaps the most powerful sex scene, though, is the first, which takes place with only partial nudity. More suggestive than explicit, it is the scene where Matty, having invited Ned home, curtly asks him to leave almost at once. He does so, then looks back and sees her standing inside her lighted hallway, wordlessly staring out at him. He paces from window to window; like the door, they're all locked. Suddenly he seizes a flowerpot and smashes one of the windows next to the door. He enters the house, grabs Matty, and they make love right there on the hallway floor. When the uproar over the movie's nudity arose among reviewers, Kathleen remarked that it pleased her that the hallway scene was the one most remembered by audiences.

Smoldering, sizzling, and *steamy* were just a few of the adjectives applied to Kathleen's performance as Matty, who explains to Ned at one point

that someone has been messing with her thermo-
stat; her body temperature always runs a couple
of degrees high. One newspaper writer, calling
her "the body of *Body Heat*," said that she wore
two costumes in the movie: One was William
Hurt and a cigarette. The other was just the cigarette. Richard Corliss, in *Time* magazine, said that
her presence in the film made it one to see "in a
drive-in, on a heavy summer night, with someone
you trust." All in all, it was an eye-catching film
debut. And although she looked supremely,
sexily confident in the movie, baring not just her
soul but also her body in front of the cameras
hadn't been easy.

At a time when some women in the film industry were making their refusals to do nude
scenes sound like the most pressing moral and
political issues of the decade, Kathleen may have
faced accusations that she had compromised her
artistic integrity by shedding her clothes to get a
part. If so, her response was certainly, "Nonsense!" She was nervous and a little scared about
the nudity and sex scenes, but she knew exactly
what she was doing—and why.

"I had read the script, of course, and I sat
down with Larry before filming began and said,
'I think we'd better talk about the nudity. I don't
want to be the token nude,' " she says. "We
talked very seriously about it and Larry described
to me how he intended to shoot each scene, and

what the camera would see. I knew exactly what to expect, and he kept his word. He was honorable with me." She has said that some scenes were cut before production got under way, although she will give no details. None of the sex scenes included in the finished movie were unnecessary, she feels, and all of them were "classy."

Kathleen also felt that "equality of nudity," as she puts it, was important. In other words, she didn't want just Matty to have to be nude all the time. After all, men take off their clothes as often as women. "Larry and Bill and I talked it out very thoroughly and agreed that we had to have an equal basis of nudity; it wasn't going to be my responsibility as the woman to show a lot of flesh and create the sexual aura. I never felt like the sex object, because there were two very cherishing, concerned men who felt just as vulnerable as I did. We all had the same vision of the film." As it turned out, the first nudity in the movie, during the credits and the opening scene, is Hurt's.

She credits Hurt's experience with sensitive scenes—he had done the famous nude running scene in *Altered States*—with calming her nerves and helping her to relax. Hurt brought not only experience but formidable talent to the role of Ned. The two got along well off-screen as well as on, and Kathleen has since said that, after costarring with Hurt, she knows how important it is for her to like the actors she works with.

Oddly, his adolescence was a wandering one, somewhat like her own. He grew up in the South Pacific, where he lived with his father, and attended college in the States and in England. He spent some time in Australia before coming to New York to work on the stage; the stage, rather than the movie studio, is still his "home."

Critics and fans have eagerly greeted Hurt as a romantic lead, a tall, blond, good-looking WASP hero. Sally Kellerman, who played with him in the PBS television movie *Verna: USO Girl,* put it more bluntly: "Now that's what I call a gorgeous hunk of man." He's not just a hunk. Marshall Mason, who directed him at the Circle Repertory, lavishes praise on his acting abilities: "generosity and anger, sensitivity and scathing sense of humor—all this and lots of sexual heat." Steve Tesich, screenwriter of *Eyewitness,* says, "His future is limited only by his ambition. If he wants to become one of the two or three male superstars, it's there for him to achieve." But Hurt says, somewhat ruefully, "I'm a character actor trapped in a leading man's body. I love character roles. I'm trained for them. I have much more fun playing them."

A philosophical man who studied theology at Tufts University in the late 1960s, Hurt has the reputation of being unorthodox in conversation and manner, not to say downright bizarre. Kathleen saw some of that side of him during the filming. "He is sometimes a little difficult to deal with personally," she recalls, "because he doesn't proceed in a linear fashion. His actions don't progress in any shape or form." In the course of one day, he could go from "needing to be supported and petted to being completely independent." When the time came to perform, however, he was completely professional.

Some of Hurt's mystical conversations with the straightforward, logical Kathleen were genuinely odd, if playful. "We'd go to dinner," she says, "and I'd spend the whole evening completely unable to understand what the hell he was talking about. I mean, it got a little scary sometimes, like spending the whole evening talking about your preferred mode of death. He said he would like to be sucked up into a jet engine and immediately atomized and I was saying, 'Oh, my God, here I am sitting with this man I have to work with tomorrow who wants to die by being atomized in a jet engine. Uh-oh.' " She hastens to add, though, "He never brought any of that stuff on camera."

On the set, in fact, he helped Kathleen deal with her newcomer's nerves. The sex scenes were filmed all at once, near the end of the project, by which time Kathleen had built up a high level of trust and comfort with Kasdan and Hurt. Still, she says, "It was rough. It's an incredible exposure, one that under normal circumstances you would never have in your life." It wasn't just being naked in public but showing Matty making love that Kathleen found difficult. She believes that sexuality is the most personal quality: "it shows how you feel about yourself, your body, your deepest values." The sets were cleared of unnecessary crew, but Kathleen found it awkward to lie naked with Hurt while technicians adjusted lighting and other production details. To take their minds off the situation, the two made up contests, like seeing who could remember more Shakespearean sonnets.

How was Kathleen affected by acting these scenes? Was she ever turned on? She admits that she was. "Part of it was very mechanical," she recalls. "Larry and Bill and I would block out the moves in advance and know what we were going to do in front of the camera, so we would be comfortable with it. And the three of us became close through the work. But you have to get over this hump. At some point, you have to kiss the other person, hug the other person. It was easier to get over that when we were alone than with the crew standing there. Then, when the tension got real heavy, we'd have races up and down the lawn —stuff like that. We'd jump into the water, just to get comfortable with each other."

She points out that the sexual excitement of her scenes with Hurt extended beyond the two actors to everyone on the set. "Everybody gets

quite excited," she says. "You look around and
the camera guys are all panting." But their excitement wasn't just sexual, she argues; the whole
team was exhilarated because they knew that top-
quality work was being done and that the movie
was going to be great. The crew's respect helped
her get through the difficult moments. Once, as
she left the set after a day spent filming a love
scene, her driver jokingly remarked, "It's about
time you got out of bed!" Recalls Kathleen, "An
older gaffer picked him up by the scruff of the
neck and said, 'You don't talk to her like that.
She's a lady.' "

The closeness on the set was supportive, but
Kathleen had to face the camera alone. After the
break-in scene, and after almost every other powerful sexual scene, she would run to her dressing
room, shaking and crying. "You can act sexuality
to a certain extent, but if you are actually being
touched, actually touching someone, there is a
gray area there, because your body is responding,
even though your mind is saying, 'Okay, now the
camera is there, I have to kiss at three quarters.'
So you're thinking that stuff, but you're also having physical reactions, because nobody can be
petted, touched, and kissed without feeling
something." Although she *did* get turned on at
times, Kathleen says that she found "Cut!" to be
"a very good cold shower." More seriously, she
adds that technical responsibility as an actor kept

her from getting too involved in the scenes. She couldn't get too carried away, because she might start rolling around and end up out of camera range.

Unlike some other women who have acted sexy parts, Kathleen is willing to admit that she works best when there's a spark of attraction between her and her leading man. Playing opposite someone who was supposed to be in love with her would be hard if she felt that he didn't find her attractive, or if she didn't find him attractive. But that attraction has limits. "You may see that actor after work and not have any desire to talk to him at all," she says. "But on the set, if you're doing a love scene, you tend to hang out together all day. You talk together and make sure you're okay. You assume an intimacy you don't have, and that works better with some actors than with others."

There were rumors that Kathleen's intimacy with Hurt was not simply an actor's pretense. The sexual nature of the movie's content, the closeness and chemistry that everyone observed between them on the set, and the fact that they were both single (Hurt was divorced from actress Mary Beth Hurt, although he was living with Sandra Jennings, of the New York City Ballet) set some tongues wagging. Did she and Hurt sleep together during the making of *Body Heat*? If so, she has been admirably discreet about it ever since, and so has he. But whether they were founded in fact or in mere speculation, the rumors hurt. One day during the filming, David Guc—with whom her romantic relationship was breaking up—said to Kathleen, "I hear you are having an affair with Larry and Bill at the same time." Kathleen's reaction: "I felt just like someone had kicked me in the stomach. It ruined something for me. And it really hurt, because every time the three of us went off to talk and to rehearse, I'd be thinking, 'Who's seeing this? What are they thinking?' It was rotten. But I realized: this is the real world."

Kathleen had made the decision not to look at rushes (daily reviews of new footage) while the film was being made. She agreed with Kasdan that, because she wasn't used to seeing herself on film, the rushes might confuse or disrupt her, making her too self-conscious to do a good job in front of the cameras the next day. She confesses that she worried a lot about how she was doing. "In the middle of the night I would lie in bed," she says, "scared to death that people were going to see one of those smoldering looks and start giggling." And so many people had told her, "The camera's got to *love* you, baby," that she went around the set asking, "How do I make the camera love me?" (She now believes she comes off well on film because she has always felt that the camera is a wonderful, flattering form of attention, "like someone looking at you all the time.") In addition to keeping her anxiety at lowest possible level, Kasdan wanted her to experience the sex scenes and the entire impact of the film in finished, edited form. When the editing was completed and she finally saw her work for the first time, she was thrilled, embarrassed, and shaken.

"It made me see what Larry and Bill were seeing in me," she says. "It was like seeing somebody I didn't know. Then there was the feeling of what other people would think, what my family would think." On the whole, though, she was proud. "I thought it was beautiful and very real. One thing I like in my work is that I've almost never seen myself pull back or apologize or try to cover something. The moment an actor starts to commit to something and then pulls back or explains it, it jolts the audience, makes them realize that they're sitting in a theater, and that's bad. I was very proud that I didn't see that in my work, even when I didn't know how it would look."

She saw the movie first in a private screening. Then, disguised in a pair of glasses, she went to a theater and watched it with an audience. "I guess I thought they were going to recognize me," she says a little self-mockingly. "Of course, they wouldn't have." Although Kathleen had taken a major risk in making *Body Heat*, this audience's reaction was her true reward. She moved two or three times during the film. At the end, she was sitting next to a woman alone. In the explosive climactic scene, as Matty and Ned approach the boathouse, the woman said under her breath, "Don't go in, don't go in!" Thought Kathleen, "This is great."

She sat in the lobby later, listening to people as they came out. "They were all arguing," she remembers. " 'She loved him.' 'No, she didn't.' Or, 'I knew she was going to do that.' 'Oh, you did not!' " Kathleen thought it was all fabulous. She followed one couple for two blocks, listening to their argument about whether Matty had really loved Ned. Her own verdict: "Yes, yes, yes! I think she was in love. I don't think she had ever had the freedom of a beautiful young lover like that." But Matty's high-school yearbook, after all, gave her ambition as "To be rich and live in an exotic land." She clung relentlessly to that ambition, whatever it cost her. Kathleen is convinced, however, that she fell in love with Ned, her dupe, along the way. Why, then, did she betray him? "Love and sex ain't necessarily the most important thing," concludes Kathleen. "That's what Matty believed."

If Kathleen had had doubts and fears about her performance or the movie in general, they were soon washed away on the tide of laudatory reviews. Everyone involved reaped praise: Kasdan as director; Danson for his deft characterization of the sharp, tap-dancing prosecutor, Mickey

Rourke (soon to make *The Pope of Greenwich Village*) for his seedy but smart arsonist, one of Ned's clients, who shows him how to set off a bomb but warns him that he isn't smart enough to do it right. Hurt, too, was acclaimed for his tortured, brilliant, and funny portrayal of Ned, lazy and self-deluded, a small-time screw-up who jogs and smokes at the same time. He starts out thinking he's in control—of Matty and their plan—and wises up agonizingly too late, as the noose tightens around his own neck.

Kathleen was ecstatic about the good notices the film received, although she has since learned that bad reviews are just as depressing as good ones are elating; she no longer takes them terribly seriously. But where *Body Heat* was concerned, one opinion in particular mattered a great deal: her mother's. To cover her anxiety about her mother's reaction to the film, she joked that the folks in Missouri weren't real big on nudity and violence. But, to her relief, her mother approved. "She's seen the film three times," Kathleen says happily. "She thinks it's terrific."

So did almost everyone else who saw it. Unfortunately, although rave reviews and word of mouth continued to draw respectable numbers to the theaters six or eight months after the film opened, it didn't become a box-office smash. High-grossing movies today must appeal to the mass market, the young audience that is more comfortable with special effects than with sensuality and prefers shootouts to dialogue. *Body Heat* may, in fact, have had more effect several years after its release than it did in 1981, through widespread availability of cable television and videocassette rentals.

But even though it didn't break any ticket-sales records, *Body Heat* became an instant classic and firmly established Kathleen Turner as a very hot new star of the highest magnitude. Everyone was watching her, and everyone expected great things.

3

The Actress with Two Faces

Kathleen, whose motto is "keep 'em guessing," did the one thing that nobody expected. She returned to New York and began turning down movie offers.

She was delighted and surprised to discover that *Body Heat* had opened doors for her. "Instead of meeting with casting directors, I began meeting with directors," she says. "They sent me scripts instead of me having to beg for them." She received four scripts almost at once.

Suddenly, she found, she was Hollywood's new femme fatale. The parts she was offered all seemed to echo what she'd done in *Body Heat*. She was pleased that they featured strong and intelligent women, and that they didn't all require her to take her clothes off ("I don't really think of myself as that kind of actress," she insisted at the time), but they had two big flaws. First, she wasn't crazy about their quality. "However important the woman seemed to be, she always ended up being an accoutrement to the man," says Kathleen. "And I found that very boring."

The second problem with the scripts was even more significant. The roles were all villainesses. "When you play a role like Matty that's so strong and evocative, people really believe that you're playing yourself and that everything else you play will be shades of Matty. It's crazy," she says. "You're an actress, you're pretending to be someone else. I wasn't Matty. I was *playing* Matty. But after just one movie, everybody had me typed."

It was a crucial point in Kathleen's career. Her first movie was showing not just all over the United States, but worldwide. In fact, Warner Brothers had sent her on a round-the-world publicity trip—no sweat for an old traveler like Kathleen—for *Body Heat*. The high point of the trip was London, where she was able to host a dinner party at Claridge's for some of her father's friends. The low point was Spain. Her wonderful voice, naturally, had been dubbed in a different language for every country where the movie was released, and it so happened that the Spanish version was particularly terrible. "That was so frustrating," she says ruefully. "I could have done it myself if I had known. I speak excellent Spanish."

Upon her return from the tour, Kathleen had

to choose: to accept one of the scripts that had been offered, or to return to stage work and wait for a part she *really* wanted. Not an easy decision, even for someone as clearheaded and decisive as Kathleen Turner. On one hand, she was broke. She says she made "not a cent" from *Body Heat*, adding with a laugh, "I would have paid them!" Friends, agents, and self-appointed advisors of all sorts warned her that if her face wasn't seen in Hollywood for a year she'd be forgotten, no matter how good she was.

On the other hand, she had a clear vision of the career she wanted to build for herself. "I had gone from doing a soap to Broadway to a film I liked," she says, "and I didn't want to spoil anything. I want to be proud of everything I do." She was convinced that doing a string of what she called "B-movie repeats of Matty Walker" would lead to an "irreversibly short" career. One thing in which she believes firmly is her ability—indeed, her right—to make choices. "I've always believed that I was in a position to pick and choose," she says. "It may mean unemployment, or that I'm going to work as a waiter. But for an actress, the only right you really have is to say no. If you ever take a job for the money, then somebody owns you."

So, refusing to settle for less than she wanted, Turner turned down every film possibility that came her way for eight long, lean months.

She did off-off-Broadway bits, she filled in on a few soap operas, she even returned for a while to waiting tables. But it wasn't altogether a dry spell for her professionally. She returned to the Arena Stage in Washington, D.C., and this time was cast, for the parts of Hippolyta and Titania in a production of *A Midsummer Night's Dream* in November of 1981.

Like her movie career, Kathleen's personal life seemed to be stalled for a time. Her love affair with David Guc had cooled, and she lived alone —except for her cat, McGee—in a tiny apartment on West 57th Street. Although she dated occasionally, she found that her portrayal of Matty Walker had had the same negative effect on her social life as on her professional options: a lot of people confused Kathleen with Matty. Some men approached her with a bit of a chip on their shoulders, as though they were saying, "Okay, lady, you're not going to put anything over on *me*." Unlike many women in the entertainment industry, she had no particular desire to date or become involved with another actor, who might have taken Matty Walker in stride. Instead, she has always been more interested in people whose lives offer some contrast to her own. So Kathleen wasn't seriously involved with anyone during this period; or, if she was, she has kept quiet about it. She concentrated on looking around for a promising opportunity to return to the screen. Finally she heard about a script with a part that she was convinced was perfect for her.

The Man with Two Brains seemed to many people to be a rather peculiar choice. It's a silly, slapstick Steve Martin farce, directed by Carl Reiner (a kingpin of Hollywood comedy ever since the days of *The Dick Van Dyke Show*) and starring Martin. The screenplay was written by Reiner, Martin, and George Gipe, who later wrote the novelization of the smash hit *Back to the Future*. In it, Martin plays Dr. Michael Hfuh-ruhurr (pronounced differently and unsuccessfully by every other character in the film), the world's greatest brain surgeon and inventor of the "screw-top method," by which a brain can be opened like an aspirin bottle—childproof, of course. He hits a beautiful woman named Dolores Benedict with his car, performs the operation that saves her life, falls in love with her, and marries her. Unbeknownst to him, however, Dolores is a conniving, gold-digging tramp who has married him for his money and her convenience. She pretends to be shy and innocent and drives him crazy by refusing to have sex with him —all the while lustily enjoying herself with everyone from the Mexican gardener to the Austrian room-service waiter.

When Michael discovers Dolores in their hotel room baring her bottom to a bearded stranger who has offered her $15,000 just to touch her behind, his eyes are opened to her true nature and he performs a "citizen's divorce." In the meantime, he has fallen in love with a gentle, sensitive, sweet woman named Ann. She is his perfect mate in every way—except that she just happens to be a disembodied brain kept alive in a jar by a not-quite-mad scientist. The campy highjinks become increasingly outrageous as Dolores plots to murder Michael, Michael searches desperately for a vacant body for Ann, and a mysterious elevator killer haunts Vienna.

Kathleen immediately saw great possibilities in the role of Dolores. "I wanted this part because it's a comedy and because the character was so outrageous. If I was very brave I could do some extraordinary things with it," she says. "It wasn't a run-of-the-mill, token female role. I thought it would be a hell of a stretch." She liked the fact that Dolores is a vampy parody of the femme fatale character she played as Matty; perhaps Dolores would give her a chance to lay the Matty stereotype to rest. "She's a send-up of Matty, a spoof," Kathleen said at the time. What better way to demonstrate her acting range than to take the *Body Heat* character to her limits, poking fun all the way?

Despite the fact that Kathleen felt she had good stage background in comedy, though, others weren't so ready to see her in a comic part. Once again, she had to fight for a role that only she believed she could play. When Reiner was told that she was interested, his response was, "She's good, but she isn't funny." He felt that a serious dramatic actress couldn't do his kind of comedy, but Kathleen insisted that he was wrong. "I got kind of upset," she admits. "I told my agent I really wanted that audition, and ultimately Reiner agreed to see me." Another version of the story has Kathleen herself saying to Reiner, "Carl, I don't care if I get the film, but I want that audition." However it came about, he agreed to let her try out for the part.

She studied the script and walked into the audition wearing what she describes as "a nice little suit." With perfect aplomb, she proceeded to do everything that the script called for. She read the scene where Dolores, who's supposed to be too weak to get out of her wheelchair, is discovered by Michael standing by the window, ogling the muscular gardener. She whirls around in surprise and falls at his feet, murmuring, "Oh, darling, I wanted to surprise you and walk into your arms tonight." Kathleen recalls: "It was just a read-through, really. Nobody expected me to throw myself on the floor. But I did—wham!— flat on my face, and then I crawled up Steve's leg. I had the offer fifteen minutes later."

Although Kathleen hadn't seen Martin's earlier movies and described her comic interests as "more Noël Coward than Carl Reiner," she liked working with Martin and Reiner. "They're hysterical," she reported. "It's the most fun I've had in years." Of Martin, she says, "He's very good to work with, very quiet and, in many ways, very reserved. He's always coming up with things. You'll be in the middle of a scene and suddenly he and Carl will have an idea that's absolutely hysterical."

Reiner and Martin had collaborated on two of Martin's earlier movies: *The Jerk*, a rambling riches-to-rags saga, and *Dead Men Don't Wear Plaid*, a spoof of detective thrillers. Most film critics now agree that *Brains* was funnier, as well as more stylish and assured, than either. Admittedly, it's a silly movie. But even the difficult-to-please Pauline Kael, who had savaged *Body Heat*, recognized that the silliness of *Brains* was inspired. Richard Schickel, writing for *Time*, called it "a Henny Youngman monologue combined with a *National Lampoon* spread" that "offers reassuring proof that the spirit of arrested adolescence lives on, at least for one more summer."

The Man with Two Brains is essentially a series of skits and one-liners. Despite some flat moments and some jokes that don't quite come off —such as the scene where Michael meets the brain of a former colleague, now residing in a gorilla's body, which could have been much funnier—there are plenty of wonderful sight gags, lines, and scenes featuring both Martin and Kathleen.

She recounted her favorite moment in *Brains* on the *Late Night with David Letterman* show: Michael drives the vicious Dolores, whom he believes to be sweet and pure, from the hospital to his house. His servants are waiting by the flower-bordered front door to greet them. She sullenly asks, "What are those assholes doing on the steps?" With a simpering chuckle, the doctor replies, "Those aren't assholes! It's pronounced 'azaleas.' I put them there for you." Kathleen got a big laugh from the audience for that one, but Letterman topped it when he quipped, "You ought to come up to the studio offices. We have lots of azaleas there."

Another great moment takes place when, addressing the portrait of his dead first wife, Michael admits that he loves Dolores, but adds: "I had the top of her head off, but that's as far as it went." He asks the picture, "If there's anything wrong with my feelings for Dolores, give me a sign." Immediately the picture begins to spin madly around on its hook, a strong wind springs up and shakes the house, a woman's voice cries, "No, no, no!" and the wall cracks. The disturbance dies down and, without missing a beat, Martin adds, "Just any kind of sign . . . I'll keep an eye out for it."

Perhaps the most brilliant sight gag in the

movie is the creation of production designer Polly Platt. In Vienna for a medical conference, Michael meets Dr. Alfred Necessiter, his rival in brain research. Necessiter offers to take Michael back to his lab and show him his revolutionary work in brain transplantation. They arrive at a modern condominium building. As Necessiter leads him down the bright, carpeted hall, Michael remarks, "You know, here in Vienna, meeting a brain scientist, I guess I sort of expected your lab to be in a castle, not a condo." "You mean," Necessiter asks as he throws open the panelled door, "something like this?" Inside is a giant, vaulted stone hallway, complete with torches, a drawbridge, even a moat with an alligator. "Leapin' lizards!" exclaims Michael. "Yes, we have those," Necessiter calmly replies, while chameleons jump across the room.

It's a mad scientist's laboratory straight out of all those old Universal black-and-white movies that show up on television at 4 A.M. The inner chamber is loaded with lobes, brains that Necessiter has kept alive in candy-colored water. He even has a coin-operated brain transplant machine, built from the guts of a video game. Here Michael establishes telepathic contact with his true love, Brain #21, whose name is Ann Uumelmehaye. In one of the movie's funniest scenes, he takes Ann's brain for a rowboat ride on the lake, affixes a pair of wax lips to her jar, and solemnly kisses them.

In a vocal joke that might have been created just to spoof one of Kathleen's pet peeves, Michael meets a beautiful blonde hooker who looks like the perfect destination for Ann's brain, until she opens her mouth and speaks with an appallingly nasal voice in a Brooklyn accent. Michael tries to work up the nerve to inject her with window fluid, the murder method favored by the elevator killer. As he hesitates, the hooker whines, "Did I blow the deal? It's my voice, isn't it? It usually makes people want to kill me." "Keep talking," he tensely orders her.

But Michael can't bring himself to kill an innocent woman. Fortunately for Michael and Ann, the elevator killer—played by Merv Griffin in a surprise cameo appearance—strikes again. He kills Dolores, leaving her bewitchingly beautiful body empty for Ann's nice-girl mind. And it's a good thing that Michael had fallen in love with Ann's mind, because she turns out to be a compulsive eater and loses her figure almost as soon as she's transplanted into it. The final scene shows Kathleen padded out beyond belief with fake fat as Michael staggers over the threshold with his bulging new bride in his arms.

Kathleen is marvelous in her zestful portrayal of the twisted, devious Dolores. She fries a prize goldfish, kicks a cat onto a Renoir canvas, teases Michael by sucking on his fingers until he's practically paralyzed with unsatisfied lust, and even tries to bake Ann's brain. She parades through the film in enough sexy lingerie to stock a Frederick's of Hollywood outlet, crooning, "Oh, I *love* to see those veins in your temples throb!" In one memorable scene, she sits in her hospital bed trying not to reveal her revulsion as Michael recites his favorite poem, a truly disgusting quatrain called "Pointy Birds," by "England's greatest one-armed poet." The height of her tricky treachery is the "suicide" attempt she stages to win back Michael's affection after learning that he's going to inherit fifteen million dollars. Clad in skintight black lace, she stands on a window ledge and moans, "I don't deserve to live," securely chained to the wall by a hidden manacle. But she gets her comeuppance after her attempt to cook Ann. Michael marches her to the door and flings her into a handy bog, crying, "Into the mud, scum queen!"

When *The Man with Two Brains* opened in the spring of 1983, Kathleen received highly favorable reviews for her clever handling of Dolores. *Newsweek*'s Jack Kroll wrote that she was "not only sensationally glamorous but also stylish and hilarious in a role that could have been nothing but long legs and lingerie. Someone," he concluded, "should give this brainy beauty more than a finger to chew on." *Playboy* called her "delicious," *Maclean's* "luscious," and *Variety* "a sizzling foil for [Martin's] comic and sexual energy." Kael proclaimed, "Turner comes alive in comedy."

There could be no doubt that Kathleen had once again brilliantly proven herself. Not only had she pulled off a demanding dramatic role like Matty Walker, but now she had demonstrated genuine comic genius. Gemini—her astrological sign and her first Broadway show—wears two faces. Kathleen had now shown her own two faces: the tragic and comic masks of classical drama, the ultimate symbol of her profession. But, although she was satisfied with her performance as Dolores, Kathleen faced some disappointments as *The Man with Two Brains* hit the theaters.

4

BODY HEAT MEETS THE DUTCH TREAT

The Man with Two Brains got good reviews but did poorly at the box office. "I'm surprised it didn't play," says Kathleen, who thought it was wacky and funny. She had hoped to reach a large audience with her portrayal of Dolores.

Perhaps audiences stayed away because they had been confused by Martin's previous films and didn't know what to expect. *The Jerk* had been a straightforward, if somewhat clumsy, comedy showcase for Martin, but *Dead Men Don't Wear Plaid* had alienated some viewers with its spliced-in footage from old black-and-white mystery movies and the many references to old films that only hard-core movie buffs understood. *Pennies from Heaven*, Martin's next movie, made without Reiner's collaboration, wasn't even a comedy; no wonder that audiences weren't sure what to expect from this volatile comedian who had first made his mark in show business with his zany "King Tut" routine on *Saturday Night Live*.

Whatever the reason, *Brains* didn't live up to expectations. Kathleen was left with some favorable notices to paste in her scrapbook, but her earnings from the film were slim. Even before *Brains* opened, however, she had made several surprising career moves: one that took her back to the stage and one that never made it into the theaters.

Her first two films had demonstrated Kathleen's dramatic and comedic abilities, her ability to exude sexuality one minute and spoof it the next. Even her most fervent admirers, though, couldn't claim that *Body Heat* and *The Man with Two Brains* had made her name a household word. But with her undisputed combination of talent, beauty, and a good reputation in the movie industry, she was poised on the brink of stardom. Had she wanted it, there is no doubt that she could have claimed the female lead in any one of the big, crowd-pleasing movies that were coming up for production in the fall of 1982, after she finished work on *Brains*. She didn't.

"I've turned down a lot of roles," she admits, "many of which have gone to Jobeth Williams and Glenn Close, who are both fine actresses and who must have seen things in the scripts that I didn't." The one part she desperately wanted, she didn't get a chance at: the starring role of the disturbed and abused starlet in *Frances*, which went to Jessica Lange. "We were finishing *Body Heat* when they were casting," she recalls, "and I couldn't even get in the door. Boy, I wanted to audition for *that* one."

After *Brains,* however, Kathleen accepted a couple of assignments that may have seemed to many like steps in the wrong direction, away from big-time Hollywood success. But Kathleen has always been determined to do things her way, which meant establishing herself as an actress *before* she became a public personality. For her, as for many other actors of her generation (including William Hurt), this serious-minded and professional approach to her work—while it does not preclude stardom—often takes the form of periodic returns to live theater. "Being in front of a camera is terrific, but that doesn't mean you can do it in front of people," Kathleen maintains. "You've got to have a live audience. That's what keeps you sane and real."

In January of 1983, therefore, she began rehearsals opposite Brad Davis for *The Toyer* at Washington's Kennedy Center. The play, written by Gardner McKay and directed by Tony Richardson, was a two-character thriller set in a cabin off California's Laurel Canyon. Kathleen termed it "a real challenge—with just two people on stage, there's not much you can hide behind." She was ready for the challenge and did good work in the play, which, however, didn't move on to Broadway as she had hoped it would. It *did* bring her back to the East Coast after several years spent mostly in California, and she was grateful for the change of scene. "To me, L.A. is getting in a car and wondering which way to point it," she joked. "I still think of New York as home."

She didn't stay home in the East for long this time. After *The Toyer* closed, she decided to accept another movie role. At this point, having played a sultry seductress and a high-camp vamp, Kathleen wanted to put the glamour image behind her. She found what she thought was the perfect opportunity to do so, in an unusual and almost unknown film called *A Breed Apart*, which might have done much to prove her depth and versatility. Unfortunately, the film was plagued with problems. Although work on it was completed, it has not yet been released.

A Breed Apart paired Kathleen with Rutger Hauer, the handsome, blond Netherlands-born actor whom *Cosmopolitan* magazine has dubbed "the Dutch treat." He first attracted the attention of American moviegoers as the rogue android whose death speech steals the scene from Harrison Ford in Ridley Scott's futuristic science-fiction thriller, *Blade Runner*. Hauer has since won acclaim for his roles as a romantic hero in two medieval fantasy epics, *Ladyhawke* and *Flesh and Blood*, and as a crazed killer in *The Hitcher*. Like others who have worked with him, Kathleen found him self-contained and a little aloof: "very strong," as she put it, "and very oriented to his own visions." In *A Breed Apart*, he was cast in an almost medieval, certainly visionary, role as a reclusive hermit and conservationist who lives alone on an island in North Carolina.

Sally Field, Jessica Lange, and Sissy Spacek were soon to create a trend of grass-roots, down-home movies about *Places in the Heart*, *Country*, and *The River*. But before any of them had so much as put on her first pair of bib overalls, Kathleen was deeply involved in playing a character as far removed as possible from Matty Walker and Dolores Benedict: Stella Clayton, a Carolina mountain woman who singlehandedly runs a fishing-supply store and mothers her young son. She also owns an island in a local lake, which she rents to Jim Malden, the hermit played by Hauer. Her son worships Malden and admires his independence, and Stella is in love with him, but the romance between Stella and Jim doesn't get off the ground until an outsider enters the world of their remote mountain village.

Michael Walker, played by Powers Boothe, is a professional climber hired by a wealthy bird-egg collector to rob the nest of a rare new breed of bald eagle that has been discovered on the island. Kathleen found the subject matter of the film, as well as its rural setting, completely new.

"I never knew there were such things as egg collectors," she said at the time. "It's tragic, these bounty-hunter characters stealing the eggs of endangered birds."

Walker is slick and smooth and an ace climber. Ascending the difficult peak to the nest, however, is easy compared to getting past Malden, who has appointed himself the birds' protector. Posing as a nature photographer, he wins Stella's friendship and uses her to get acquainted with Malden. In an unexpected reversal of character, Walker saves Malden when he is threatened by a group of angry hunters; he then changes his mind about stealing the eggs. The eagles go free, but the plot fizzles out.

Despite original music rather surprisingly contributed by Maurice Gibb of the Bee Gees, stunningly lush cinematography by cameraman Geoffrey Stephenson, and the natural beauty of the backwoods location, *A Breed Apart* had big problems in its story line. Stella's background and situation are never clarified, nor are Malden's. Their relationship remains murky; although they make love, the audience is never sure how they feel about one another, or why. Walker's change of heart is unexplained and the movie limps to a meaningless conclusion.

When it finally premiered at the Cannes Film Festival in May of 1984, *A Breed Apart* wasn't well received. But Kathleen, Hauer, and Boothe got credit for giving it their best try. Said *Variety*, after criticizing the film's lack of reason or dramatic tension: "The three leads have a hopeless task of fleshing out thinly developed roles despite their charisma." And, while "Audubon would be proud of the effort," the same review continued, "the producers should be prepared for the worst." Presumably Hemdale-Sagittarius, the producers, came to the same decision, for Orion Pictures has never released *A Breed Apart*. Although fans of Turner and Hauer would doubtless be interested in their performances, the studio executives have apparently decided to write the film off as a loss. Unless, like Michael Walker in the picture, they have a change of heart and release it (possibly on videotape), *A Breed Apart* is destined to remain a film unknown.

After work on the film ended, it was back to New York once again for Kathleen while she looked around her for the next project. Her professional reputation was growing steadily—and so was the "Kathleen Turner mystique."

By this time Kathleen had become something of a mystery woman as far as the public was concerned. The image that built up around her was compounded of many ingredients: the comparisons to older stars that *Body Heat* had evoked, her own impatience with stereotypical Hollywood practices and attitudes, her insistence upon personal privacy, and her aloof behavior that could sometimes verge on arrogance or abrasiveness.

Although it had been a smashing debut, *Body Heat* had colored everyone's reactions to Kathleen, not always in ways that were favorable or comfortable to live with. Columnists and publicists looking for a "hook" or an image for Kathleen were influenced both by the sexy femme fatale role and by the multitude of allusions that had been made to screen goddesses like Astor, Hayward, and Stanwyck. It was easy for not just the public but also people within the entertainment industry to pigeonhole her as "glamorous," "sultry," and "mysterious." Kathleen had successfully overcome Carl Reiner's preconceptions about her acting to win the part in *The Man with Two Brains*, but even a satiric spoof of the femme fatale couldn't entirely dispel the image.

Kathleen has made no secret of her dislike for the Hollywood environment, the world where people "do lunch" and seem to end every conversation with, "Love ya, babe." She feels that many Hollywood actors lack depth, and she has said so. Such attitudes, together with her refusal of roles that typecast her as a modern Mata Hari, gave her Hollywood reputation a touch of the rebel or maverick. And although she has always been willing to help promote a play or film she's involved in—as in the promotional tour she undertook for *Body Heat*—she avoids rather than seeks opportunities to get her name in the headlines and her picture in the tabloids. Newspaper and magazine readers remain ignorant of her diet, her beauty secrets, and her love life; most do not even know whether she is married or not. Kathleen believes that her life offstage or off the movie set is nobody's business but her own, and in the first years of her movie career she was especially emphatic about that belief, rejecting most requests for interviews and appearances.

"I'm not one of those actresses who is consumed by her career," she said shortly after finishing *A Breed Apart*. "And that's why I enjoy living in New York. In Los Angeles I always feel like an actress. In New York it's not like that. There the private person is just as important as the public person, and that's the way I like it. The first I know about a role is when my agent calls to tell me about it. I haven't read about it in the trades or heard a lot of gossip about who else has been up for it. There's another thing," she added. "I find that men in the East are a little more courteous to women. And I have strong ideas about how men should behave to women."

Her notions about appropriate male behavior are of a piece with other of Kathleen's strong ideas. She has been called something of a snob or an elitist, and she admits that she doesn't pretend to like people she can't tolerate; she was brought up in a protected, exclusive environment in

American communities abroad and she absorbed some of the values of that way of life. As another result of her cosmopolitan upbringing, she is contemptuous of anything she sees as smallmindedness or provinciality—an attitude that does not always win admirers. The young New York actress who attended Southwest Missouri State several years behind Kathleen, for example, says that she still hopes to run into her in the Village sometime and tell her what she thought of Kathleen's sarcastic appraisal of SMSC and Southern girls in a *Playboy* interview.

Although some of her opinions are quite acid, however, Kathleen disdains gossip, refusing to dish out titillating anecdotes or opinions about her colleagues as adamantly as she turns away most questions about her personal life. Reiner, who describes her as "top of the crop" professionally, admits that she doesn't always come off as the most likely contender for this year's Miss Congeniality award. "Some people on the set found her a little acerbic because she's very quick, doesn't have time for slowness," he says of the days they spent together filming *Brains*. "Some found her cold because she's private, aloof because she's quiet. But, boy," he adds, "when she's called upon to do what she's supposed to do, you realize she's not aloof at all. I think she's just very concentrated."

Kathleen attributes her ice-princess reputation in some quarters to two things: her way of speaking and her desire to avoid personal entanglements on the job.

As regards her speech mannerisms, some of her apparent coldness may be a result of the careful training in grammar and diction that is characteristic of English schools. She says: "I don't use slang a lot and I don't go, 'Hey, man,' and 'OK' and 'Like, far out.' I speak very properly and formally, even though it comes off stiff and arrogant. When I was starting auditions, I was terribly nervous, so I would be so incredibly proper it was ridiculous. And I would get feedback from the agency like, 'Who is this prima donna? We don't need to waste our time on this.'"

Kathleen also believes that it's very important for a lead actor or actress to be friendly with a stage or film crew, but not *too* friendly. "You *want* to have friendships, to be available to everyone," she says. "You know everybody's name on the set, you try to know if they are well or if they are sick." Many of her colleagues have praised Kathleen's "trouper" mentality, her ability to remain briskly cheerful even during difficult weeks of shooting on location. But she is careful not to become too involved in relationships that could affect work, not to take sides in quarrels and disputes, and especially not to put herself in a position where a friendship with a man could lead to misunderstandings—on his part or anyone else's.

"You're the girl, you're the star, and you can't go down to the bar and just have drinks with the guys and stuff like that," she asserts, "because there's always that question of sexuality involved. Especially if you're on location and everybody is away from home, you're going to make all kinds of trouble. One nymphomaniac in this position could turn a crew upside down and sideways. You have to be aware of your position and use it responsibly."

She admits that she's a great flirt, although her flirtation, like her friendships with the crew, has strict limits: "I enjoy flirting. It cheers the guys up, it cheers me up; I like it a lot, but I'm more careful now to say, 'Aren't I a terrible flirt —ha, ha.' I make sure they know that's what it is, because I don't want to hurt anybody." It may be, however, that her casually flirtatious manner fails to endear her to some of her colleagues—particularly the female ones—and thus supports the image of Kathleen Turner as cold and arrogant.

The Kathleen Turner mystique included plenty of contradictions. For every rumor of difficult behavior on a set, there was an interviewer who wrote convincingly of her warmth and charm. For every turn-down to a would-be interviewer, there was an act of kindness to a crew member or public praise of a colleague. Like her career, Kathleen's public personality seemed somewhat mercurial and chameleonlike. For the

most part, however, she didn't concern herself
with favorable or unfavorable publicity. Instead
she prepared herself for the next acting challenge.

Having played both the serious and the hysterical sides of the classic screen vamp and followed them up with a character study of an
Appalachian mountain woman, she was, as always, ready for something *different*. She found it
in an offbeat romantic adventure film that was the
surprising spin-off of a controversial publishing
phenomenon. And once again she had to fight for
the role. But the astounding success it was to
bring her would make it, in the words of one
reviewer, "the last role she'll ever have to fight
for."

The romance-novel market was the liveliest
part of the entire publishing industry in the late
1970s and early 1980s. Initially a small venture of
Canada-based Harlequin Books, the romance
business grew and grew as women snapped up
hundreds of the packaged, standardized, and san-
itized love stories. Soon rival publishers entered
the field, and more romances appeared under
such series names as "Desire," "Ecstasy," and
"Rapture." Passion-hungry shoppers could
choose from among literally thousands of slim,
almost-identical books (numbered so that fans
could make lists and avoid buying books they'd

already read) marketed by Harlequin, Silhouette, and other romance lines. If these weren't enough, there were also the heavy hitters of the genre: the so-called "bodice-ripper" novels, big, thick romances with flowery lettering on their covers and pictures of passionate beauties, usually with their bosoms about to fall out of their clothes, being embraced by Clark Gable look-alikes. Readers couldn't get enough of them, it seemed. In some years romances accounted for nearly half the paperback books published in the United States.

They presented a superficial variety. Some were squeaky-clean and old-fashioned, some were steamy and practically soft-core pornographic. Some were set in St. Louis in 1978, some in Timbuctu in 1897. But all shared a common formula: girl meets man, sparks fly, they have some reason to hate or detest one another, hatred turns to love, and love conquers all. There was nothing new about the story; what was new was the amazing surge in the number of these romances being written and read.

The romance phenomenon quickly became a controversy. Publishers claimed that churning out large numbers of profitable romances brought in money that enabled them also to publish books of greater literary merit but lesser sales appeal. College English teachers decried the romances' one-dimensional characters, predictable plots, and frequent lapses in grammar; fans declared indignantly that they were inspiring or that they saved marriages. No sooner did a feminist or psychologist attack their stereotypical portrayal of women as weak-willed and man-hungry than a female lawyer or executive defended them as relaxing entertainment that only a simpleton would take seriously. Some people called them "trash"; others "good, clean fun." And a thirty-three-year-old waitress in Malibu, California, saw the possibilities in a story that could capitalize on the romance industry and satirize it at the same time.

Diane Thomas was a native of northern Michigan who had graduated from the University of Southern California. She worked for several years as an advertising copywriter and then, fed up with the commercial life, decided to pursue her dream of a career in show business. She studied under acting teachers Sherman Marks and Jack Garfein and performed for a while in improvisational theater before returning to writing, not advertising copy this time, but her first screenplay. Like Larry Kasdan and Kathleen in *Body Heat,* Thomas showed that beginners sometimes do have what it takes. Working as a waitress to pay her bills, she wrote a script called *Romancing the Stone,* a delightfully ironic view of adventure and love from the point of view of a romance novelist.

In 1979 Thomas's screenplay came to the attention of actor and producer Michael Douglas, who eventually bought it for $250,000—not bad for a first script by a rookie writer. It was to earn hundreds of times that much, but only after Douglas had spent years turning it into a hit movie.

Douglas had a reputation for taking as much time as he felt was necessary to make his projects successful. By the time he turned his attention to *Romancing the Stone,* he had established solid credits on both sides of the camera. He was determined not only to produce but also to star in *Romancing*—although, as it happened, his leading lady emerged from the picture a superstar and outshone her leading man.

Michael Douglas was born in 1945 to Kirk Douglas and English-born actress Diana Douglas. After his parents divorced and his mother moved to the East Coast, he attended first a military school and then Choate, the prestigious eastern preparatory school. When it was time for college, however, he said no to Yale and yes to the University of California in Santa Barbara. A true child of the 1960s, he dropped out of school to meditate on a commune for a year, then, after another year spent learning the show-business ropes in Europe as a second assistant director on three of his father's films, he returned to Santa Barbara and majored in drama. He was named the school's best actor and its best director. He also spent three summers at the Eugene O'Neill Memorial Theatre Center, where his twenty-year friendship with Danny DeVito—who played the incompetent thug Ralph in *Romancing the Stone*—got started.

Having decided to act, Douglas also decided to test himself the hard way: instead of letting his father's connections give him an easy break, he put in several years studying with Wynn Handman of the American Place Theatre and working in off-Broadway productions in New York. He also did some television work, including "The Experiment" for *CBS Playhouse*, which won him his first film contract. After a series of capable performances in forgettable films (*Hail, Hero; Adam at 6 A.M.; Summertree;* and *Napoleon and Samantha*, a Disney film with Jodie Foster), he was cast as Assistant Inspector Steve Keller in ABC-TV's *The Streets of San Francisco*.

Executive producer Quinn Martin picked Douglas for the role because the show's star, veteran actor Karl Malden, happened to be in Martin's office when Douglas came in to audition. Douglas hit it off so well with Malden (whose wife, thirty years earlier, had suggested to an ambitious young actor that he change his name from Isadore Dempsky to Kirk Douglas) that Martin signed him up immediately. The good relationship between the two on-screen and off helped make *Streets* a hit. But after four years, although Michael had received three Emmy nominations and had directed two episodes of the show, he was ready to move on.

Kirk Douglas had owned the film rights to *One Flew Over the Cuckoo's Nest*, Ken Kesey's cult novel of anarchy and repression in a mental hospital, since 1963, when he had appeared in the Broadway stage version. Now Michael decided to produce the movie. Getting backers for the project, which many viewed as too depressing and bizarre to be successful, wasn't easy. But, says Douglas, "I had fallen in love with a book and I wanted to see it made as good as possible. I saw it through for five years." His faith in the project was justified. *One Flew Over the Cuckoo's Nest*, starring Jack Nicholson, was 1976's big hit—the first movie in forty years to win all of the top five Academy Awards. To date, it has made more than $200 million worldwide.

He took his time with his next production project, too, spending three years to make *The China Syndrome*, in which he costarred with Jane Fonda and Jack Lemmon. He then acted in *Coma*, with Genevieve Bujold, *Running*, with Susan Anspach, *It's My Turn*, with Jill Clayburgh, and *The Star Chamber*—all the while developing properties for his own new production company, Michael Douglas Productions. After four years of preparation, he was finally ready to begin work on the first two of these new projects. One was *Starman*, a science-fiction romance directed by John Carpenter, with Douglas as executive producer; it earned a third Academy Award nomination for actor Jeff Bridges. The other, with which Douglas was much more intimately involved, was *Romancing the Stone*, to be directed by Robert Zemeckis.

Despite his frequent good-natured denials, Michael Douglas bears an extraordinary resemblance to his father: six feet tall and ruggedly handsome, with green eyes, sandy blond hair, even the famous cleft in the chin. He cast himself well as Jack Colton, the roguish adventurer of *Romancing*, who roams the jungles of Colombia looking for a fast buck. He knew, however, that Jack, while vital to the action, humor, and romance of the story, wasn't its real hero, and Douglas had no intention of making Jack's part more important. As Kathleen later said, "I don't think Michael is one to judge a script by how big his part is. Besides," she added, "he gets to swashbuckle."

Jack was colorful, but for *Romancing the Stone* to work, Douglas had to find the perfect actress for the challenging role of Joan Wilder, the shy romance novelist who is catapulted into real-life adventures wilder than any faced by her intrepid heroine, Angelina. Kathleen heard about the part and wanted it, but Douglas and Zemeckis turned her down. Determined to play Joan, she persisted. In a career studded with daring choices and smart moves, it may have been her smartest move yet.

5

JOAN OF THE JUNGLE

Kathleen got hold of a copy of the *Romancing* script, and her initial interest in the part increased. "Here was a character who was not only at the very center of the story, but it was a movie *about* her," she says. "I was so sick of getting scripts where I was supposed to be hard and sexy just to make the male lead look sympathetic. Here was a script where the changes the woman went through were the focus of the story."

Steven Spielberg's *Raiders of the Lost Ark* appeared the year before *Stone*, and most critics and reviewers compared the two. The obvious similarities—slam-bang action sequences, hidden treasure, an exotic location—have a Spielbergian touch, not surprising because director Zemeckis, a graduate of the University of Southern California's Cinema School, was a Spielberg protégé. In fact, Spielberg had produced two movies written by Zemeckis: *1941* (with John Belushi and Dan Aykroyd) and *Used Cars* (with

Kurt Russell and Jack Warden). Zemeckis learned much about chase scenes from his mentor, Spielberg; he puts his actors through their paces at breakneck speed (one disgruntled critic wrote that Zemeckis has "the finesse of a demolition-derby entrepreneur").

The differences between the two films, however, are greater than the similarities. For one thing, while *Raiders* tried successfully to capture the spirit of the adventure serials of the 1930s and 1940s, *Romancing* deliberately spoofed the whole notion of escapism even while it offered a perfect example. Even more significant, however, was the difference that Kathleen had recognized. Both films were romantic comedy adventures, but *Romancing* had a twist: the hero was a heroine. In *Raiders,* the Karen Allen character was little more than an uneasy appurtenance to Indiana Jones's quest, an extra something for him to rescue when he got tired of chasing after the Ark of the Covenant and a consolation prize when he lost it to the federal bureaucrats. In *Romancing,* Joan Wilder *is* the story. It's not just a "women's movie," though—the action and humor have plenty of appeal for male viewers and for kids. But the comedy is more sophisticated and the love story wittier than those of *Raiders* because the character of Joan Wilder is given some depth and allowed to grow and change.

Part of the interest Kathleen felt in the part

was due to its range and lightness, qualities she was eager to display to a wider audience than had seen her in *Body Heat* or *The Man with Two Brains.* Part of it was also her identification with Joan, an unmarried thirtyish woman who lives alone in Manhattan with her cat, Romeo. Kathleen, too, was unmarried and living alone in a sublet apartment in Manhattan. Her cat's name was McGee, not Romeo, but she saw elements of herself in Joan; she says that the nervous, ordinary-looking Joan of the early scenes, who pads tearfully around her apartment in a plaid bathrobe and socks after finishing her latest lusty epic, is "one of the only scenes I've done that's as small as I am." It was an opportunity for her to create two opposite aspects of a personality in one picture: first the plain-Jane author, dreaming of an ideal romantic hero, and then the hidden heroine, the sexy, vine-swinging Joan of the Jungle. Chameleon that she is, Kathleen couldn't fail to want the role.

Michael Douglas and Robert Zemeckis, however, didn't think she could handle it. As she explains it: "They knew I could pull it off when Joan has her adventures in South America and really blossoms. But they weren't sure I would be convincing as an introspective sort of homebody, which is what she is at the beginning of the picture." Says Douglas, "The hit you get from Kathleen is confidence. The only question was the vulnerability of the opening." As she had done twice before, Kathleen fought to change the preconceptions that threatened to keep her from being cast. She flew to Los Angeles to test for the part.

Although it's considered unusual for a proven actor to agree to a screen test or audition after the first film or two, Kathleen didn't hesitate. When it comes to laying her acting abilities on the line, she is no prima donna. "I don't think it's insulting to be asked to demonstrate the side of yourself that others haven't seen," she says, adding, "It must have gone well, because I got the role." With the casting completed and Thomas's finished script in hand, Douglas and Zemeckis began shooting and *Romancing the Stone* started to take shape. But Douglas's qualms about Kathleen's ability to handle the unglamorous early scenes were not totally without foundation.

"We had a little struggle in playing her down in the beginning," he recalls, "in getting her to trust us. She felt a need to protect herself, how she looked, and a lot of people have said, 'My God, this is the girl from *Body Heat*?' Now she realizes how important it was in terms of that whole transformation working. The arc of the movie is based on the growth of this character."

The film opens in a Western cabin, where the final scene of Joan Wilder's new book is taking place. We hear a woman's voice, the author's, providing commentary; she's actually writing the scene as it happens. The audience's first clue that this film isn't going to take itself too seriously comes when the unshaven villain menaces Angelina with, "You can die quick, like the tongue of a snake, or slow like molasses in January," and the author's puzzled voice says, "But it was October." Angrily, the villain replies, "I'll kill you no matter what month it is!" (In one of the many clever but subtle touches that pull the film together, Joan's real-life enemy, Colonel Zolo, uses a similar quick-death, slow-death question at the end of the film.)

After Jesse, Angelina's mysterious, Clint Eastwood-like hero, disposes of the villain's three brothers with three perfect shots, the two lovers meet. Because the most hackneyed image of lovers meeting in romance fiction is to have them running toward each other across a meadow, Angelina and Jesse dismount from their horses while they're still a good hundred yards apart and go leaping and bounding over the sagebrush and tumbleweeds toward each other. Then, as they ride into the sunset on Jesse's horse (with a saddlebag full of gold on Angelina's), the scene fades to Joan Wilder, headphones blaring schmaltzy matinee-movie music into her ears, hair caught up into an untidy bun, tears streaming down her face, typing "The End."

The brilliant opening does two things. It pokes gentle fun at the fantasies of romance fiction, and it sets up the very funny contrast between Joan's beautiful, adventurous heroine and Joan herself. In her emotional reaction to her own story (it may or may not be true, but most romance publishers like to say that only someone who believes in the stuff can write it well), Joan shows that she takes the clichés of romance seriously. Her attempts to make the people she meets in the course of her adventures act according to the "rules" of romance fiction give the movie its ironic flavor.

Later that same day, Joan receives a package in the mail from her brother-in-law in Colombia; he has recently been killed in a particularly messy way, so she figures he must have mailed it just before he died. She also receives a shock when she discovers her apartment vandalized. To top it off, her sister, Elaine, calls from Cartagena, Colombia, and tells Joan she's being held hostage by a criminal gang (headed by Zack Norman and Danny DeVito). To save her sister's life, Joan must bring the mysterious package to Cartagena immediately. Joan isn't a seasoned traveler—as her publisher (well played by Holland Taylor, familiar to television audiences as Ruth from the short-lived sitcom *Bosom Buddies*) puts it, Joan gets motion sickness on the elevator at Bloomingdale's—but she's game. She sets off, and a wacky chain of events is set in motion.

Pumps, a linen suit, and a large, heavy suitcase aren't very likely equipment for an adventure, but then, Joan isn't expecting an adventure. With not one but two groups of bad guys (government *and* private enterprise) after her, however, she is sidetracked onto the wrong bus and stranded in the mountainous jungle. Again the movie gets in a dig at conventional romance fiction: the dark, moustached, handsome Colombian who mysteriously appears on Joan's bus (played with just the right comic blend of suavity and violence by Mexican actor Manuel Ojeda) is exactly the sort of character with whom a heroine would fall in love in a Harlequin novel, but here he's the number-one villain. He tries to kill Joan. She's rescued by a scruffy, greedy, cynical bum named Jack T. Colton—the *T,* he assures her, stands for *Trustworthy.* Jack, played by Douglas, isn't really all that interested in helping Joan (he rescued her from Zolo only by accident) but finally, in desperation, she offers him $375 in traveler's checks to guide her to the nearest telephone. "American Express?" he asks suspiciously. "Of course," she replies. "Lady, you've got a deal," he says.

Their adventures begin. They slog through torrential tropical rainstorms, slide pell-mell down a mountainside on an avalanche of mud,

After a stint in a soap opera and a Broadway debut, Kathleen sizzled onto the screen as Hollywood's hottest new femme fatale.

In *Body Heat*, Ned Racine (played by William Hurt) thinks he's cool enough to handle Kathleen's seductive Matty Walker...

...but she leads him into a web of mystery, deceit and murder in the great tradition of *film noir*.

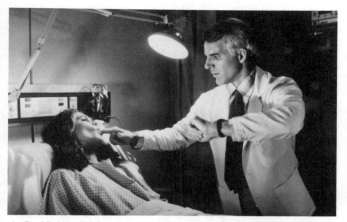

As Dr. Michael Hfuhruhurr, *The Man with Two Brains*, Steve Martin lusts after his sexy patient—until he discovers she's a heartless gold digger who's only interested in his bank balance.

Jack Colton (played by Michael Douglas) is having a hell of a good time, but timid novelist Joan Wilder isn't enjoying her trip to Colombia in *Romancing the Stone*.

Between the mud slides, car chases, and gun battles, Jack and Joan find time for some *Romancing* of a different sort.

In an amazing professional tour de force, Kathleen creates the split personality of *Crimes of Passion*: by day she's buttoned-down dress designer Joanna Crane, who dreams of a normal relationship with an electrician portrayed by John Laughlin...

...and by night she's a hooker called China Blue, tortured by the ravings of a deadly street-corner preacher played by Anthony Perkins.

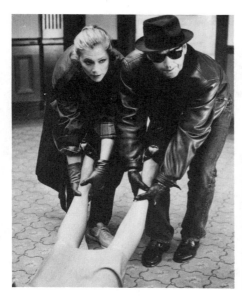

In *Prizzi's Honor*, the family that slays together stays together. Helping her hit-man hubby Charley (Jack Nicholson) dispose of the body is just part of the day's work for Irene, the hit woman-turned-housewife.

Irene turns her charm on Mafia leader Don Corrado Prizzi (played by William Hickey) in a desperate gamble to hang onto Charley, the money she stole from the mob, and her life.

Romance writer Joan Wilder thinks she's finally found the hero of all her fictional fantasies...

...but reality isn't always a dream come true, as Jack (Michael Douglas) and Joan discover in *The Jewel of the Nile*.

Critics hailed *Peggy Sue Got Married* as a classic for Kathleen's portrayal of a middle-aged woman who relives her high-school years with all her adult memories intact.

dodge potshots from Colonel Zolo's not-quite-crack troops, swing across a deep river gorge on vines *à la* Tarzan, face down a village-full of hostile drug smugglers, drive a car over a waterfall, and more. Along the way, Joan gets rid of her little one-drink sample liquor bottles and learns how to swig from a quart of whiskey like Jack. She undergoes a transformation like that of Katharine Hepburn in *African Queen*—a stiff spinster lets her hair down (literally) and discovers her own humor, strength, and sensuousness. As her clothes get grubbier and grubbier, Joan gets sexier and sexier, and Jack gets more and more determined to steal the map she carries. To Joan, the map is the ransom for her sister's life; to Jack, it could lead to the big score.

One of the delights of *Romancing* is the way in which Joan's romantic ideals keep colliding with reality. She beams with gratified relief at Jack, who finally conforms to her notion of proper manly behavior and relieves her of her enormous suitcase, but her smile turns to an expression of shocked outrage when he hurls it over a cliff. Later she berates him for not looking at her when she talks, until he calmly reaches out with his machete and chops off the head of the snake that had been creeping up behind her.

In a clever parody of the typical sitting-under-the-hair-dryer-eating-bonbons romance reader, Jack and Joan, looking for a telephone, find trouble in a small village populated by drug smugglers. Their backs are literally up against the wall, and Jack snarls, "Write your way out of this one, Joan Wilder!" Suddenly, the vicious-looking thugs, hung about with guns and knives, are all smiles. It turns out that Joan Wilder is their favorite author, and their leader, goofily portrayed by Alfonso Arau in one of the movie's funniest bit parts, reads aloud to them from her books every Saturday.

Kathleen shows Joan blossoming into a smiling, dimpled beauty in the central love scene, where Jack buys her dinner in an outdoor cafe and teaches her to dance in the plaza. She dances shyly, yet with grace, "like a woman who didn't know she could," as one reviewer wrote. Later Jack makes love to her and convinces her to find the treasure herself rather than turning the map over to her sister's kidnappers. It's obvious, however, that he has other plans for the treasure; romance is part of his plan for getting to the secret of the map, which turns out to be a gigantic emerald. Says Danny DeVito as Ralph, a hoodlum from Queens who is comically ill suited for jungle derring-do, "At least I'm stealing the stone like an honest thief! I ain't trying to romance it out from under her." As it happens, Joan winds up on one side of a river with the map, and Jack is on the other with the stone. He agrees to meet her in Cartagena, and she's left wondering if he planned to steal the stone from her all along.

Joan's newfound resourcefulness and bravery, as well as Jack's integrity and innate heroism, are put to the test in the dramatic confrontation scene at the old fort. It's night. The two women, the crooks from Queens, and Colonel Zolo and his sinister squad—with Jack under guard—all try to get their hands on the stone. Zolo succeeds, only to have the hand holding the stone melodramatically chomped by a crocodile.

Joan engages in a desperate battle with the one-handed Zolo and cries out to Jack for help. What fictional hero ever faced such a dilemma? He can either keep his grip on the tail of the croc, which is on the brink of vanishing (emerald and all) into the ocean, or he can rescue the girl. While he wrestles with the problem (and the reptile), Joan valiantly fights off Zolo, whacking him on the stump with a two-by-four and then setting him afire. Jack makes the approved good guy's decision, but by the time he arrives on the scene the heroine has saved herself and there's nothing left for him to do. An opportunist to the end, he kisses her goodbye and dives into the bay, either to escape the police, to catch the croc, or both. Joan is left in the lurch, something that would *never* happen to Angelina.

If *Romancing* were nothing more than a satire of romance fiction, the movie would end there.

But it is both a satire and a romantic fantasy in itself, with a few more twists than Joan Wilder's books but with the same basic happily-ever-after story. The movie ends where it began: in New York, with Joan finishing a new book, one that tells of her South American adventures but adds a last-minute reunion with the hero. In "real life," however, Joan's still alone, although her jungle sojourn has changed her from drab and mousy to confident and hopeful. Her confidence is justified one fine day when she rounds a corner to see Jack and his new sailboat—the *Angelina*, under full sail—on the street in front of her apartment building. Like Angelina on Jesse's horse, she climbs aboard and they sail into the sunset together, down West End Avenue.

That sailboat scene posed plenty of problems for the filmmakers. The crew waited for the breeze to die and kept the sails furled until the last possible minute, for fear the boat would actually begin to move. But it was the least of the technical problems Douglas and Zemeckis faced in making an adventure movie on location. The location was Mexico, not Colombia, but the jungles, the rain, and the mud were all too real.

Romancing was a very *physical* film, and Kathleen and Douglas did many of their own stunts. Since his *Streets of San Francisco* days, Douglas had enjoyed doing his own action scenes when he could. When not working, he keeps busy skiing, flying, riding motorcycles, and sailing. He used to race cars, until he spun out and totaled his Lotus at Willow Speedway. Former tomboy Kathleen says, "I get a kick out of doing my own stunts whenever possible."

One scene that Turner and Douglas did without stunt doubles was the famous mud-slide sequence, in which the side of a slippery hillside collapses in a downpour and launches a screaming Joan on a dizzying plunge straight down, through trees and underbrush, into a pool of muddy water. Jack follows an instant later and bellyflops into the pool, face first into Joan's lap; he looks up, shakes the water and mud from his eyes, and exclaims, "What a ride! I'm tellin' you, this has turned into one hell of a morning!"

According to Kathleen, Douglas insisted on realism in this as in every scene. The actors were mounted on wooden sleds at the top of the hillside, the camera was positioned above them on another sled, and they waited for the inevitable daily thunderstorm to begin. As first Kathleen and then Douglas shot downhill on a carefully prepared but concealed track, the crew stood by to supplement the rainfall with 150 gallons of mud and water, which they threw liberally on the stars. The scene ended with the two coated from head to toe with muck. Kathleen recalls, "We got to the point where we just started laughing hysterically." The breathless action and decidedly

unromantic mud-slinging of the scene, which is
funny in the way that a good cream-pie fight is
funny, made it a favorite for television and theater previews. It was the clip most often shown in
promotional appearances for the movie, as when
Kathleen brought it to *Late Night with David Letterman* in April of 1984.

Back in 1983, though, work was still under
way in Mexico, and many members of the crew
experienced that vacationer's malady known vari-
ously as Montezuma's Revenge, the Mexican
Two-Step, and the Tourist Trots. Kathleen
didn't have one sick day, perhaps because she
had lived in Venezuela years earlier. "I may have
built up an immunity from living down there,"
she speculates. "But a Mexican told me that if I
had a good shot of tequila and ate one jalapeño
pepper every day, I'd be fine. Luckily, I like that
stuff."

Before the filming was completed, the physical exertions of her role had gotten one of Kathleen's legs badly cut and cost her stitches in the
head and one arm. She remained undaunted and
did everything that was asked of her. Douglas
says, "Her trouper mentality was really inspira-
tional. We were in a war down there making this
picture—tremendous logistic, weather, and production problems—and she was so supportive. It
was like finding an emerald in the rough, a real
and grateful discovery." Kathleen says, more

matter-of-factly, "I went to high school in England, and the attitude there is that acting's a job. It's not nine-to-five, but you have certain responsibilities." She admits, though, that she got "pretty tired of being wet for fourteen or fifteen hours a day," and she expressed a desire for her next film to be "something dry. A nice picture that we can film in a studio somewhere that's good and warm and dry."

True to her practice on earlier films, Kathleen didn't watch the daily rushes as *Romancing* was being made, and she refused to speculate about its potential success or failure. "I'm short-sighted that way," she told an interviewer who asked whether she expected the movie to be as successful at the box office as romance novels were in the bookstores. "I don't think in terms of commercial projects. I don't even see rushes. I don't know if it's a film until it's finished." Although she couldn't be sure until it was finished, she was making a film in which everything—acting, dialogue, setting—was excellent, but she was at the center of it all, delivering every look and every line perfectly.

She first saw the movie at a Dallas press screening, along with her mother and her grandparents from Springfield. "My mother loved the movie," Kathleen reported proudly afterward. Mrs. Turner asked about the film's rating and was pleasantly surprised when Kathleen told her it was PG (open to all ages, with parental guidance suggested). Both *Body Heat* and *The Man with Two Brains* had been rated R (restricted admission).

As for Kathleen herself, she couldn't help but be pleased with the flood of overwhelmingly positive notices she received after *Romancing* opened in March of 1984. In *The Village Voice*, Andrew Sarris called her "the most exciting enchantress to zoom out of Hollywood since Jessica Lange" and added, "One might say that a star is born when one begins mentally casting her for everything in sight. And so it is for me with Kathleen Turner at this moment in film history." Richard Schickel, writing in *Time*, described her as "the kind of treasure everybody in Hollywood should be filching a map to discover." *Cosmopolitan* called her "a latter-day Lombard"; *People* claimed she was "terrific"; *Playboy* said she had fulfilled her early promise; *The Washingtonian* said she was "dynamite." *The New Yorker*'s Pauline Kael, while lukewarm about the movie in general, agreed that Kathleen's performance was "exhilarating." *Newsweek* said, "It was hard to remember exactly what Turner looked like in *Body Heat*. After *Romancing the Stone*, it's impossible to forget."

The same *Newsweek* review asked a question that had occurred to many moviegoers: Why does Douglas like misleading titles? Some people thought that *Romancing the Stone* sounded like a sword-and-sorcery film, another Conan adventure or perhaps a King Arthur epic. What did it mean? The obvious reference, of course, is to Jack's attempt to seduce Joan into giving him a chance at the map. But there is a more specific meaning, which Kathleen explained in her first appearance on the Letterman show. " 'Romancing a stone' is a jeweler's term," she said. "It means making a cut in a raw gemstone to bring out the heart of the stone." The heart, naturally, isn't just El Corazon, the heart-shaped stone at the end of the map; it also refers to Joan's and Jack's spirited and loving hearts, "brought out" by their unlikely escapades.

What about those legions of romance readers, the ones who would probably buy Joan Wilder's novels *Treasures of Lust* and *Angelina's Savage Secret*? How did they feel about a movie that professed to be about a romance writer but gently mocked its own subject matter? *"Romancing the Stone* hit a vital nerve with romance readers," says Kathryn Falk, publisher of *Romantic Times* newsletter and spokesperson for the romance publishing industry. "The film was the first opportunity for readers to see their fantasies on the screen, and, since at least half of the readers dream of being a romance writer, the film fulfilled more than one fantasy." She adds, "Most romance readers grew up on Nancy Drew books. Kathleen Turner is every grown-up's version of the new Nancy Drew, with an extra fillip of sex appeal and physical beauty." And as for Douglas, the annual convention of romance readers and writers sponsored by Falk's newsletter gave him 1984's Romantic Hero of the Year award.

"It's three years this summer since *Body Heat* came out," Kathleen reflected as *Romancing* was released. "That was my first movie and an important one for me, obviously, but fortunately it wasn't such a wild success that I got shot into orbit. I say 'fortunately' because truthfully, if it had, I wouldn't have known how to behave. Whereas, if *Romancing the Stone* does as well as everyone seems to think it will, I'll be able to handle the situation. I've learned quite a lot during the past three years."

Romancing not only lived up to everyone's expectations, it surpassed them. It was one of the blockbuster hits of the summer and lingered in the theaters for many months. A large number of viewers saw it more than once. It became the ideal first-date movie, perhaps because, as one psychologist conjectured, everyone hopes that a first date will turn into an adventure and a lasting relationship, and *Romancing* expressed those hopes in a playful way. Whatever the reasons, it was undoubtedly a megahit. Less than three years after her movie debut, Kathleen Turner had become an undisputed superstar.

6

ROMANCING THE STAR

"Kathleen can do it all," said Michael Douglas soon after *Romancing the Stone* was released. "She's funny, sexy, vulnerable and endlessly intriguing, because you never know which side she's going to show you next. It's obvious she's going to be a big star."

Others shared his conviction. *Romancing* was followed by a flurry of newspaper and television interviews that Kathleen forced herself to carry out in order to promote the movie. Because *Romancing* was such a crowd-pleaser, she received much more public attention than had come her way after *Body Heat* (which had impressed the critics more than the ticket-buying public). She admits that, true to her Gemini nature, she had mixed feelings about her sudden celebrity.

On the one hand, her essentially private nature was pleased that she hadn't yet achieved the kind of instant recognizability that bedevils long-time stars like Barbra Streisand and Robert Red-ford (as well as products of media hype like Joan Collins and Mr. T). "I can still get through a supermarket without being recognized, and that's okay with me," she said several times during the summer of 1984. "I'm not after a flash success. I'm building a career. I mean to be around for fifty or sixty years."

But on the other hand, she wouldn't have been human if she hadn't taken a childlike but genuine pleasure in at least *some* of the trappings of success. In April she clearly had fun with her glamour-girl image when she sashayed onto the set of the Letterman show wearing a black minidress and a lot of leg, adorned with black stockings and spike heels (she was greeted by a chorus of wolf whistles from the audience). And in June she treated herself to a showbiz status symbol. "Possessions don't mean a lot to me," she said. "But there is one possession that makes me feel that I've made it. I bought a 1970 Mercedes-Benz 280SL. It's a little convertible, a real classic, the rounded one they made before they made the one that looks like an elephant. When I ride around with the top down and people look at me, I say to myself, 'I bet they think I'm a movie star.' It makes me feel . . . *wow*. I haven't had a car in eight years. This is my big splurge." It's a typical Kathleen Turner contradiction that, after enjoying one of her anonymous trips to the supermarket, she would want to carry her groceries home in a "movie star" car.

While recognizing the dangers of success, Kathleen feels that her unusual childhood has helped her steer clear of them. "It makes a difference that I never grew up with any sort of veneration of these worlds—movies and television. Not living in the States most of the time never made these things too important to me," she says. "It's not better than my real world. A lot of people think that this world [movie stardom] must be amazing and mystical and God given and you can have anything you want and it solves all your problems. In fact," she goes on, "it eases some things and creates a whole batch of problems."

Always level headed and practical, Kathleen worked to keep the positive and negative aspects of her success in perspective. "Being a star is a lot harder than just being an actress," she admitted. "A star has power, and power can hurt people. I have to be very careful of what I say and do. On the other hand, it's terrific to have people invest in me, to have all that energy and support flowing toward me and carrying me along." As the months went on, however, she began to wonder whether it was carrying her in the right direction. She was concerned that public attention might become more important to her than personal relationships based, as she says, on "real love and admiration." So she began seeing a therapist, a woman to whom she fondly refers as "my shrink."

"I went to her because I had this concept, this feeling that there was a capital-*K*, capital-*T* Kathleen Turner who was getting a lot of attention and was more important than I was," Kathleen now says. "And I was feeding her! I was spending my time trying to perform this Kathleen Turner, and I thought, 'This is *sick!*' And I felt it was getting very dangerous. If I couldn't sit at home and be happy reading, if I had to go out and get my dose of attention every day, then I was going to be in trouble."

Kathleen credits her shrink with helping her separate her life and her work. "She has really helped me find a perspective," she says. "Now I will go perform Kathleen Turner when I should, when I have to—at an opening, when I'm on the set—but I don't want to feed my energy into this public figure every day. I want to live my own life." Kathleen continues to see her New York therapist from time to time when she's home between films.

Her growing celebrity may have posed problems for Kathleen, but one problem she didn't have to face was lack of work. As her career gained momentum, she was bombarded with scripts and offers. After *Body Heat*, she had felt compelled to reject roles because they were poor-quality repetitions of what she'd already done. Not so now—she was so hot that the biggest and the best wanted her. "It's nice," she said. "I'm starting to be offered more and more good roles. It's not so much a problem of me having to go out and prove myself each time around." But Kathleen doesn't like to coast along on the momentum of earlier successes; she doesn't have to prove herself each time around any longer, but she insists upon growing with each role. And believing as she does that "the reward of success is not money, but relief from the pressure of having to take every job," Kathleen once again looked for a project that would stretch her talents and give her the opportunity to create a new screen persona.

Not long after *Romancing* was finished, she made the most controversial choice to date in a deliberately unconventional career. She signed up for the lead role in Ken Russell's lurid tale of sex and psychosis, *Crimes of Passion*. Fresh from her first PG film, a box-office success that established her as a wholesome, mainstream, all-American star, Kathleen was about to appear in the most explicitly and violently sexual movie to play in America outside the triple-X porno houses. She faced disapproval and condemnation from family, friends, feminists, and film critics. And in deciding to do *Crimes of Passion*, she also risked destroying a new and special love affair.

Since breaking up with David Guc (who remained her agent), Kathleen had maintained a low-profile love life. Unlike many rising stars (or would-be celebrities), she was never snapped by the paparazzi while being squired around town by an actor, senator, or punk rocker. Nevertheless, her sexy roles and on-screen chemistry with costars William Hurt and Michael Douglas had given rise to the usual rumors of fooling around on location. (In the case of Douglas, who is married and a father, at least one New Yorker claims to have spotted the two stars necking feverishly on a coast-to-coast flight after the filming of *Romancing*.) But whether Kathleen and her leading men engaged in casual affairs or not, certainly they were never acknowledged publicly as important relationships.

Not that Kathleen wasn't interested in having a relationship. "I was getting to be rather well known and my career was starting to open up," she recalls. "I had the leisure to attack this whole New York dating scene. I thought of becoming a sort of socialite and went on about five dates. I absolutely hated it. I'm no good at dating." Being a beautiful and glamorous star, she adds, is no guarantee that you'll always have something to do on Saturday night. She admits that she spent some frustrated nights sitting alone at home, thinking, "Why isn't anyone here? I'm *gorgeous* tonight!"

Kathleen had had a problem, after *Body Heat*, with men who acted as though they expected her to try to trick or manipulate them. Now she found herself meeting men who had a different preconception of what a "date" with Kathleen Turner meant. She explains: "I would find myself calling them up at six o'clock before a dinner engagement and saying, 'Listen, if you think anything is going to happen after dinner, forget it.' 'No, no, no, I just wanted the pleasure of your company.' Right. Sure. Eleven o'clock and you're still trying to shove him out the door. I was very flustered. I decided that that was not going to be my way of life. It had a little to do with *Body Heat*. People expected me to be very glamorous and sensuous and perhaps even easy—who knows?"

Monogamous by nature, Kathleen kept looking. She learned how to deal in cold, practical terms with the impetuous infatuations that can beset a lonely young woman who happens to work with some of the most desirable men in show business. "I used to have this thing that I'd sort of fall in love for ten days," she confesses, "but I knew that I'd do that, so I'd say, 'Don't do *anything*. Don't go have dinner with him. Don't do anything during these ten days, because something could happen.' Then, sure enough, after the end of ten days, I'd turn around and think, 'Yeah, he's a great guy, but the craziness is gone.' I was looking for somebody, so every time I met someone I was very attracted to, I had that 'What if?' " As she told one interviewer, she didn't want a dashing rogue like Jack Colton. "What I'm looking for," she laughed, "is a man who will share the burdens but not get in the way when I'm working." But by the time she gave out this description of her ideal man in the spring of 1984, she had already met him. Ironically, she met him through Guc.

His name was Jay Weiss. They met in October of 1983, when Kathleen came home to New York from the filming of *Romancing the Stone*. Many actors, riding high on their first big commercial success, buy a house that demonstrates their place in the Hollywood community: a beachfront "cottage" in Malibu or a redwood-and-hot-tubs country place in the Canyons. Not Kathleen. "Home" to her still meant New York—but she *was* ready for a change of address.

She was still subletting her "tiny room" on 57th Street. "One morning I woke up unhappy and decided to grow up and get myself a decent place to live," she says. As any New Yorker knows, finding a good apartment in Manhattan is harder and more heart breaking than finding buried treasure in South America, even for a movie star. But Guc's assistant happened to know Jay, an entrepreneurial young real-estate developer who owns several apartment buildings in Manhattan and has interests in at least two realty companies. She asked Jay to help Kathleen find a new place.

"At first, he refused," Kathleen continues. "He said he didn't do that kind of thing. But she bugged him, and finally he lined up a bunch of apartments and took me to look at these buildings, none of which I liked." She wound up moving into an apartment in the Chelsea district of New York. It was modest and comfortable, with only three "movie star" props: a leather director's chair with her name on it and two outstanding George Hurrell black-and-white photographs of Kathleen (one showing her with Michael Douglas). Otherwise, she kept the decor simple, highlighted by a sofa of dusty-rose leather. The chief accessories most of the time seemed to be books (usually two or three in progress at once) and tapes.

Kathleen may not have liked any of his apartments, but she took a shine to the realtor. "I turned out to be a nice guy," says Jay, "even if I'm a landlord." Kathleen took him to lunch at the Russian Tea Room to thank him for his efforts, and the two wound up talking until four in the morning. "After that, I think every single night I was in New York, we went out together," she says. "At first, he didn't want to . . . well, get involved with an actress, so I had to persuade him. He couldn't resist me," she adds, laughing at the Matty Walker-type line.

Kathleen was attracted to more than Jay Weiss's undisputed good looks (he's almost exactly her age, handsome and stylish, with dark hair and eyes). After dealing with men who found her too forceful, opinionated, or independent, she found Jay's self-confidence refreshing. "He's one of the few men near my age who has such a strong sense of himself that he doesn't have to incorporate his woman into his identity," she says. "It's crazy, 'cause we're from totally different backgrounds, but in some ways we're the same person, with the same values and reactions to things."

One reaction they had in common was the decision not to move in together. "I'd done that," Kathleen says, referring to her years with David Guc, "and I didn't understand why I wanted to live with the man instead of marry him, but I knew I didn't want to get married. And Jay had lived with somebody like that as well." With both of them sure they didn't just want to live together, Jay and Kathleen began to think about marriage, even though they had known each other only a few months. In February of 1984 they went to Paris together.

"That was the real test," recalls Kathleen, "because we knew we would be together every minute for ten days." The relationship must have passed the ten-day test, because Jay proposed in March, and Kathleen accepted.

Kathleen credits the success she'd achieved in her work with enabling her to say "yes" to Jay, something she wasn't ready to do with David Guc. "I think I've reached a certain level of self-confidence and feel different about myself. A couple of years ago, all my attention was focused on proving things to myself and others," she says. "At that point, you don't have the confidence to make a commitment like marriage. You have to get that out of the way first. I couldn't have gotten married—and I think my husband feels the same way—until reaching that certain point of confirmation."

She was also convinced that in Jay she had found a man who would be supportive when she needed him and still give her the freedom to pursue her career. Some actors have claimed that they prefer relationships with other performers, because people outside the industry don't understand the strains and stresses of the actor's life. Kathleen doesn't agree. And although Jay is in the real-estate business, Kathleen describes him as "not just your basic businessman at all." Having had a musical career of his own and produced several off-off-Broadway shows, he is familiar with the entertainment industry.

"He understands the demand I'm under; he can share it with me when I come home," Kathleen claims. "On the other hand, it's relieving not to have my work be the center of the world." Earlier in her career, during her relationship with Guc, she had reveled in the fact that her work was of central importance to both of them. She now feels that "you have to have another place to go, and Jay gives me that. I get very tired sometimes."

Both Jay's respect for Kathleen's work and her freedom to make independent choices were put to the test early in their relationship. By the time they had gotten serious about one another, Kathleen had agreed to do *Crimes of Passion*—a decision she is sure many men wouldn't have been able to accept.

In *Crimes* Kathleen took on one of the most bizarre roles in any recent American film: a woman who by day was an uptight, ultraconservative dress designer named Joanna Crane and by night was a flippant, foul-mouthed hooker named China Blue, who had a different costume and a different fantasy for every man who could put up fifty dollars. The movie wasn't to be a sentimental, prettified view of the seamy side of life, in the style that the French call *nostalgie de la boue;* instead, it was a sweaty satyricon, complete with whips, handcuffs, and stainless steel dildoes. Massive sections of the original version were cut and the film was reedited four times before the motion picture industry's ratings board would remove its X and give it an R.

Why would an actress who clearly had it made take such a chance? What made Kathleen so eager to accept a role that might have meant career suicide?

Kathleen admits that her choices of roles don't depend on what she calls "the whole literary value" of the script. She tends rather to respond to the character, to the technical challenges it would present, to her importance in the screenplay. She wants to do films in which her part is crucial, a pivotal part of the action and meaning, not merely an ornament. Beyond that, she looks for a character who "essentially tries to make her own rules in a way, not just a pattern of behavior that's given to her but something she creates herself." In Joanna/China Blue, she found a character who was desperately breaking society's rules to try to heal her inner wounds. In some ways, the role was the logical next step for Kathleen, the ultimate Gemini, a single character in which Kathleen would have to combine two personalities, two sets of characteristics as different as possible. It was the opposite of *Romancing*, in which Joan's adventures gave her a chance to develop her hidden qualities; in *Crimes* Kathleen would have to take two sides of a tragically fragmented personality and try to weld them into one believable performance.

"I've noticed that I keep playing characters who are themselves acting, that is, who are presenting an idea of themselves to someone else," she said. "I also like to play women who are vulnerable, who display their own emotions and feelings without the protection of a mask." *Crimes* was the perfect opportunity to explore the themes of game playing and vulnerability in the harshest, most intimate terms.

Ironically, the very popular success that seemed endangered by *Crimes* is one of the factors that made Kathleen do the film. "The part was an acting tour de force," she explains, "and you don't get offered too many of those, especially if you are becoming a commercial Hollywood leading lady. Studios don't want you going out on a limb and risking your reputation with that kind of role, because you might lose audience. As time goes on and you become more popularly successful, the odds are you start to be limited in your choice of roles. So I really thought it was a good time to grab it, because I thought I would act my ass off in it. In one scene she's a chippie with a whole closet full of clothes and characters—the southern belle, the stewardess. And then the character goes back to real life and you have to play it straight. I love the acting on acting on acting."

Another reason Kathleen was eager to do *Crimes* was the opportunity it gave her to work with controversial British director Ken Russell. Although she generally doesn't select a part based on the big names involved—she's more concerned with compatibility and whether she likes a director than with how many hits he's made—she feels that Russell is "one of the great directors" and that making a movie with him would help her career. "I had wanted to work with him for years," she says. She was, however, concerned about his reputation for being temperamental and difficult to work with. "If somebody yells at me, I can't work," she explains. "I can't yell back, I just close up. So I met him and we communicated really well." Despite some later disagreements, she found Russell "funny and witty and nice," and she now feels that his reputation is to some degree undeserved.

Russell, in turn, wanted Kathleen for the part, as did screenwriter Barry Sandler, who says that she was "by far the first choice for the role." They wanted her not because of the sensual allure she had displayed in *Body Heat* or the box-office success of *Romancing*, but because they had loved her in the all-but-forgotten *Man with Two Brains*. There's not much humor on the surface of *Crimes of Passion*, but Russell and Sandler agreed that some of China Blue's scenes with her clients called for the comedic timing and flair Kathleen had demonstrated as Dolores.

So Kathleen accepted the part, against the

advice of many people who cared about her and her career. Jay was "very concerned"; her mother was "appalled"; even David Guc had "very mixed feelings." By the time she and Jay decided to marry, though, she was already committed to the project, and she felt that others close to her would simply have to understand and respect her ability to make her own decisions. "I don't go to my mother for advice on what films to do," she says rather tartly. She also admits to a streak of perverse stubbornness. "In a way," she now says, "all those people telling me not to do it almost made me decide that I must. I had one week when I changed my mind and tried to get out of it, and realized that I couldn't and shouldn't. It's very hard for my mother to understand, but that's not why I do it, and I can't let that tear me up."

She went ahead with the project, with some protection in the form of contract clauses. After reading Sandler's original script, she realized that it couldn't be shot the way he had written it: "It would be quadruple-X," she claims. Her contract demanded that the film must receive an R rating or not be released, that there would be no full nudity, and that she had the right to direct any scene that she felt was questionable. As it turned out, she had to invoke her right of direction only once.

Crimes of Passion is essentially a four-character morality play, with Kathleen on screen most of the time. The other characters are: the "Reverend" Peter Shayne, a psychotic derelict and street preacher who becomes obsessed with China Blue, embarks on a crusade to "save" her soul, and ultimately identifies his own tortured sexuality with her pain; Bobby Grady, a former high-school football star stuck in a dull suburban marriage who stumbles across Joanna's secret life, makes love to her as China Blue, and finally persuades her to try letting a man into her daytime existence; and Amy Grady, the faded, waspish wife Bobby leaves for Joanna.

All three are really only exaggerated symbols, caricatures almost. Despite some attempts to breathe life into the role of Bobby, he comes across like the others: not real people but events and conditions that affect Joanna/China Blue. Annie Potts and John Laughlin are well cast as Amy and Bobby Grady, and Anthony Perkins, as the "Reverend," gives a garbled but urgent reprise of his most famous role, the knife-wielding Norman Bates of *Psycho*.

In such films as *The Music Lover*, with Richard Chamberlain as the composer Tchaikowsky, Russell had demonstrated his fondness for sensationalistic images, headlong pacing, and bombastic dialogue. *Crimes* was no exception. Sandler's script was rich in vivid but vague rhetoric, as when Shayne exclaims to China Blue, "You wear your anguish like a breakaway chastity belt!"

(Perkins spits out this and other, even more awkward, lines so quickly that one reviewer conjectured, "Russell must have held a gun to his
head.") The film proceeds in a series of confron-
tations: tired, passionless arguments at the Grady
home and fervid, profane screaming matches in
China's room in the wonderfully seedy Paradise
Hotel. What some filmmakers might have treated
as a painful but sensitive exploration of human
sexuality, Russell gleefully turns into a searing
freak show.

The story of *Crimes* is simple. It's a more
frenzied, more explicit version of the Sadie
Thompson story, filmed as *Rain* with Joan Craw-
ford in the title role. Joanna Crane, a frigid work-
aholic by day and whore by night, meets two men,
each with a plan to save her. Shayne spies on her,
buys her time and then lectures her, and threatens to kill her. Bobby treats her nicely, makes
love to her, and threatens to move in with her.
The love of a good man penetrates the defenses
Joanna has built around her emotions, and she
falls in love with Bobby. But just when she decides to abandon China Blue's sexual masquer-
ade, Shayne comes along to put her out of her
misery with a razor-sharp giant dildo. In the final
costume act of the movie, he puts on China's
cheap blue dress and platinum wig and dresses
her in his priest's uniform. When Bobby breaks

in to save her, she kills Shayne to save Bobby's life. At the end of the movie, it's not clear whether Bobby and Joanna will live happily ever after, but at least they're having good sex in the meantime.

Throughout the film, China Blue is shown catering to a variety of her customers' sexual urges: she dresses up like Miss Liberty to perform oral sex on one man; she lets another chase her down a dark alley and "rape" her by prearrangement (after telling him that her father raped her when she was a child). Kathleen was able to function during these scenes by distancing herself from her character and blocking out the potential effect on the audience. "I suppose I have a kind of blindness where I don't see the effect on someone else," she says. "I just see the work. I see what I want to do with it."

The only scene that she found hateful to do —one that still disturbs her—is the notorious sadomasochism sequence, in which China dresses in leather, handcuffs a young cop to her bed, and has sex with him while images of police brutality are shown in brief flashes on the screen. While she doesn't whip him, her heels rowel his thighs like spurs, drawing blood, and, in shots that were edited out for general release but appear on the unrated videocassette recording, she sodomizes him with his nightstick. Afterward, shaky and trembling, China tries to make a joke as she unlocks the cuffs, and the cop spits in her face. "It's China Blue's turning point, when she decides to stop being a whore," Kathleen says, justifying her decision to complete the scene. "So it's right for the film, but awful to do—makes you hate yourself. The payoff is when he spits in her face and she's got that scene in the bathroom when she's crying and trying so desperately to put makeup on and pull herself back together, when she knows she's not in control; she's been fooling herself the whole time about this whore character being free. So that's worth it."

Kathleen was forced to invoke her contract only once during the filming of *Crimes*. When an older woman hires China Blue to make her dying husband "feel like a man again," Barry Sandler wanted Kathleen to play the whole scene naked. She refused. "It was ridiculous," she says. "In the first place, everybody's going to be wondering when she'll put her clothes on, so nobody's going to be listening to the words. I want them to listen to the scene instead of look at my body. Secondly, from all I've read about prostitution, nudity is a gesture of trust and intimacy and they just don't allow it. If they take off their clothes, they're just another woman." According to Kathleen, Sandler was frustrated about the number of changes that had been made in his screenplay and wanted to humiliate her, but she stuck to her guns and said, "Talk to my lawyers." Eventually the scene was shot—with Kathleen wearing skimpy blue underwear.

Clothing and costume are vitally important throughout *Crimes*. The clothes she wears are symbols of the character's split personality—gray flannel by day, sleazy rayon by night. They also helped Kathleen create mannerisms and voices, in *Crimes* as in her other films. She builds a character by establishing physical traits: "How does she walk? Does she wear high heels? The shoes really affect the whole attitude. Matty, in *Body Heat*, wears high heels and a tight skirt; she's a woman who's always touching herself, touching her hair, checking her face, touching her thigh. In *Crimes of Passion*, Joanna wears flat shoes and jackets and ties, so you've always got constriction in the neck and nothing to push you forward in a feminine manner, which is what heels do, so she's always a little lumpy."

Kathleen made a field trip to Frederick's of Hollywood in the course of creating a physical image for China Blue. She bought five-inch heels and the little plastic bag that bounces off China's hip as she struts her mean streets. "I put the purse on," Kathleen reveals, "and started to feel the character. My legs and hips felt different. She's just throwing it out there. I made her real loose at the hips. Her legs kind of swing. You get the feeling of 'screw you,' because that's what her body's doing. So I find that first, and then the voice that the body produces. Joanna's is pretty tight and talks-like-this. China Blue is 'like, oh, yeah . . .' "

She did her homework for the film in other ways, too. She read studies of prostitutes and discovered that most of them are motivated by the feeling she had sensed in Joanna/China Blue: not lust but anger. She learned that "prostitutes hate and despise men almost entirely and make a man pay for his pleasures as a kind of revenge. So I knew that Joanna was a very disturbed and angry woman." And she admits that she drew upon a personal reservoir of anger to portray Joanna.

"Every few years or so, I get a build-up of anger, of *something*," she says. "You've been fulfilling all your goddamned responsibilities, you've been forging ahead, and yet every few years there's a whole body of anger that you haven't tapped. You've just let it sit. It was one of those times when *Crimes of Passion* came along."

As she had done for Matty Walker in *Body Heat*, Kathleen humanized Joanna by making up a past for her. At one point China Blue tells Shayne that while she was in the kitchen trying to make her husband's favorite casserole, he was in the bedroom making her best friend. Like the remark about incest, it may or may not be true, but it gave Kathleen an understanding of Joanna's anger. "I envision that Joanna was trying to be Superwoman," she now says. "She was carrying this job and this marriage, and when they were breaking up, her husband turned around and said something like, 'You're not a real woman.' It's a problem for so many women today. What do you do? Do you spend your time making sure your man is all right or pursuing your career? And Joanna got burned! I envision that one night she went out and bought that wig because it was her idea of the absolutely grotesque, the absurd, and she went out to see if any man was going to pay attention to her. She got into the control thing and liked it. It was obviously a very destructive way to use her anger, but it was her first access to it."

Kathleen admits to being disappointed in the finished film. "It's not as good as I wanted it to be," she says, "but I'll stand by my work. I think it's good." Critical opinion generally agreed with her. The movie took a trouncing at the hands of reviewers who found it "terminally silly" (*New York*), "reckless" (*Time*), "limited and incoherent" (*Playboy*), and "sentimental" (*Newsweek*). Kathleen's performance, however, was hailed as a genuine classic, a "clever, daring, and mad" achievement. One critic wrote that she was gutsy and gallant; another said, "The fact that the role is hooey doesn't stop Turner from putting everything into it." Said Richard Schickel, "It's a dangerous performance, but she never falls off the high wire—even when the rest of the movie hits the tanbark."

The controversy that arose over *Crimes of Passion* had less to do with its cinematic merits or lack thereof than with its sexual violence. It appeared in the autumn of 1984, as did Brian de Palma's parody of the porn-film business, *Body Double* (which quickly became notorious for the scene in which a woman is lengthily murdered with an electric drill); in some cities, the two premiered on the same day. Together they provided a double helping of ammunition for those who wanted to take aim at permissive pornography passing as art. Russell added fuel to the fire with his furious references to "Lola Mincemeat," as he dubbed a female member of the ratings board who had insisted on many of the cuts in the film.

The furor over ratings doesn't seem to have boosted the take at the box office, as some reviewers speculated it might. *Crimes of Passion* did poorly in the United States, perhaps because some theater-owners refused to book it. Released as *China Blue* in Europe, where Russell has a large following, it was a big hit. Today the unrated version—complete with the nightstick scene—is a popular videocassette rental and has become something of a cult classic in the U.S.

Kathleen feels that there is "some good basis" to believe that movies like *Crimes of Passion* encourage sex crimes, but she says quite bluntly, "I actually wasn't very concerned with that. I don't see films as real. It's my job." She was more concerned with the movie's effect closer to home: on Jay and her family.

She and Jay were married in August of 1984, after the filming of *Crimes* and before it was released. He wasn't happy about the movie, feeling that it was exploitive and brutal, but he admitted that it was a superb acting challenge. Once work was complete on the film, she arranged a private screening for the two of them. After watching it, they went to a restaurant to talk it over.

"It was very rough on Jay, very upsetting to see the nudity or see another man kiss me or touch me," Kathleen recalls, and jokes, "I guess I'd have felt bad if he hadn't felt that way, if he'd said, 'Oh, that's fine, darling.'" Jay's real problem wasn't jealousy, she continues, but the sense that their privacy had been invaded, that someone was watching *them* on the screen. "I'm showing an intimacy that in most normal lives is never seen outside the bedroom," she says. "Why would anyone else ever see someone's wife in that position?"

Her family feels the same way: "They just see 'Kathleen' all the time, whether I'm acting or not. They think somebody's going to see it and think I'm a whore, which never enters my mind." Kathleen's mother is especially horrified at the possibility that, because Kathleen is so good at *acting* like a whore, people will be convinced she really *is* one. A theater manager in Springfield arranges special previews of all of Kathleen's films for Mrs. Turner—all but *Crimes of Passion*, that is. Kathleen's mother has never seen it and, says Kathleen, "she never will."

As for herself, Kathleen is very matter-of-fact about separating what she does on the stage or screen from her real-life activities and feelings. "That's an actor's protection," she maintains, but adds, "I'll think twice about doing another film like *Crimes of Passion* because of its effect on Jay." Jay isn't the only one who might be affected by a similarly explicit film in the future: Kathleen and Jay plan to have a family, perhaps soon, and as even a fiercely independent thinker like Kathleen concedes, "If you have kids who have to go to school and explain it to their friends, you think differently about what you do." Possibly to give her kids something to boast about in show-and-tell session in years to come, Kathleen topped off *Crimes* by taping a children's special called *Loving the Rock*, a lighthearted musical spoof of *Romancing* in which she costarred with a gang of puppets.

In her response to the good reviews she received for *Crimes*, Kathleen showed a cool awareness of that two-sided quality of success that is sometimes summed up in the phrase "the bigger they are, the harder they fall." "Success is great, but at the same time there lurks the fear that you have got to fall on your face sometime. I thought it might be *Crimes*. I actually thought I might get killed over *Crimes*. I was happy with my work, but I wasn't sure other people would see what I wanted to put into it. But if you don't take chances . . ."

Kathleen took a couple of big chances in 1984—marriage and a potentially disastrous film role—and didn't fall on her face once. In fact, she was still a star and shining more brightly than ever.

7

Hit Parade

Seldom has a major American actress given bravura performances within one year in two such disparate films as *Romancing* and *Crimes*. As 1984 drew to a close, Kathleen's name began to be linked with that of a prominent Hollywood gentleman: Oscar. She was widely expected to receive an Academy Award nomination as Best Actress.

The nomination didn't materialize. One source claimed that a split vote kept her from competing—ballots were cast for *Romancing* and for *Crimes*, but neither received the necessary number. "It would have been a nice recognition, but it doesn't change anything," said Kathleen philosophically. "There was a lot of talk about it, which was nice. People noticed."

Among the people who noticed were the folks who give the Golden Globe awards and the Los Angeles Critics' Circle awards. Kathleen won both for her performances in the two films jointly. By the time she received them, she had already completed work on *Prizzi's Honor,* which was filmed in New York and California in the fall of 1984 and released in the summer of 1985.

Although she has been in the movie business for a relatively short time, Kathleen has worked with some of its best actors and directors. *Prizzi's Honor* paired her up with two heavyweights: Academy Award-winning actor Jack Nicholson and veteran director John Huston, whose first film was *The Maltese Falcon* (1941). A sardonic look at a Mafia romance, *Honor* baffled some viewers—and at least one of its stars—but delighted critics and most audiences. It became the prestige hit of 1985.

The story of how Huston came to make *Prizzi's Honor* is itself almost as complex as the plot of the film. In early 1984, relaxing at his villa in Puerto Vallarta, Mexico, after finishing *Under the Volcano,* Huston came across a set of galleys of Richard Condon's 1982 novel, *Prizzi's Honor.* Condon had sent the galleys two years before, thinking that the director would enjoy the echoes of *The Maltese Falcon* the book contained, but they had been misplaced and Huston had never seen them. Huston and Condon, both of whom lived in Ireland for part of their careers, had known each other for thirty years. Huston had helped get Condon's first book, *The Oldest Confession,* made into the 1962 film *The Happy Thieves,* with

Rex Harrison and Rita Hayworth. He also appeared in the 1974 film version of Condon's *Winter Kills*.

Condon, perhaps best known for his 1959 book *The Manchurian Candidate*, which was filmed in 1962, has specialized in pointing out the dark sides of the American dream. His style, like those of Joseph Heller and Thomas Berger, has been called "paranoid surrealism," a label he cheerfully accepts. In *Honor* he gives a warped version of the old Horatio Alger story: "Charley Partanna ultimately marries the boss's daughter," he says. "In that way it's an all-American fairy tale about success." In a variation that Alger probably would not recognize, it just so happens that Charley's boss is the ruthless Don Corrado Prizzi, head of an organized crime family, and Charley is a hit man instead of an ambitious mail clerk. An outraged student of Mafia activities, Condon grew up in a poor neighborhood and watched gangsters at work. "It has long fascinated me to see some people just go in and take what others worked so hard to get," he says. Instead of a biting denunciation, however, *Honor* takes the form of a tongue-in-cheek satire that gets in a few digs at M.B.A.s as well as Mafiosi.

As soon as he'd read the galleys, Huston lined up producer John Foreman, who had worked with him on *The Man Who Would Be King* and other films, and bought the movie rights.

Janet Roach, a screenwriter who had written a
profile of Huston for public television, just happened to be visiting the director in Puerto Vallarta, and he asked her to collaborate with
Condon on the script (which remains very close
to the book). Meanwhile, Roach had already sent
Huston a copy of *Prizzi's Honor* because she
thought he might be interested in acquiring the
film rights. Once the screenplay was under way,
Huston began casting the film, using his preferred method: "As I'm reading, I think of the
person I know who is most like the character, and
then I think of an artist who is most like the person I know. Sometimes they're the same person."

He assembled a formidable line-up of talent
on both sides of the camera: Nicholson as the
oafish but shrewd Charley, torn between loyalty
to his *padrone* and love for the woman who
cheated the "family"; Kathleen as Irene Walker,
the blonde California "tax consultant" and free-
lance assassin who captures Charley's heart and
a big chunk of the Prizzis' money; Huston's
daughter Anjelica, Nicholson's longtime lover, as
Maerose Prizzi, who has been cast out from the
family for cheating on Charley but schemes to
win back not just her place but also her former
fiancé; acting coach and character actor William
Hickey, who endured a day-long screen test and
was made up to look thirty years older in order
to play Don Corrado Prizzi; John Randolph, who

was blacklisted for years during the McCarthy era, as Charley's "Pop"; and Robert Loggia and Lee Richardson as the Prizzi sons, Eduardo and Dominic. As Amalia Prizzi, the don's sister and housekeeper, Huston cast Ann Selepegno, a retired director's assistant and family friend who had never acted. At first reluctant, she finally agreed to play the part. "When I read the script, I knew why he wanted me," she says. "The map of Italy is on my face." (Later she summed up her acting debut by remarking, "I can't say I ever felt like Sarah Bernhardt, but it was fun.")

Huston wanted Nicholson for the part of Charley Partanna from the start, but Nicholson couldn't make up his mind about the script. He took his time deciding whether or not to do the picture, which in turn created an agonizing delay for Kathleen. She says: "John couldn't understand why, after several readings, Jack was still troubled by the script. He said to him, 'It's a very funny story. What's wrong with you?' Jack said, 'What? It's a comedy?' He had never seen it as a comedy. He read it again and said, 'Holy shit, this *is* funny!' The producers wouldn't confirm that I had the part until they knew they had Jack. They didn't know whether or not they had Jack for months. I turned down another film because it would have been a conflict. I finally had to call Jack and say, 'Hey, guy, give me a hint.' The next week, he agreed to it."

The technical crew of *Honor* was like a who's who from Huston's long Hollywood past. Film editor Rudi Fehr had worked on *Key Largo* in 1948; script supervisor Meta Wilde had worked on *The Maltese Falcon;* director's assistant Monique Blanke was the daughter of Henry Blanke, who had produced *The Maltese Falcon* and *The Treasure of the Sierra Madre* (the latter co-starred Walter Huston, the director's father, who won an Academy Award for his performance).

Careful and imaginative use of location is a hallmark of Huston's films, and in *Prizzi's Honor* the emphasis was on authenticity. The impressive opening wedding scene (slyly undercut by a shot showing the nervous groom, half a head shorter than his bride in the best *Godfather* tradition) was filmed at the Church of St. Anne and the Holy Trinity in Brooklyn Heights. A somber mansion on nearby Pierrepont Street was selected as the eighty-four-year-old don's home. Nothing could have provided a greater contrast to the dinginess of Brooklyn than the sumptuous Bel Age Hotel off Sunset Boulevard in Los Angeles, where Charley and Irene meet for their first date. Her California home is all soft pastels and silky fabrics; his Brooklyn apartment is functional black and white.

One of the most important members of the team was production designer Dennis Washington, who worked with Huston to create the

slightly unsettling quality of temporal vagueness
and anachronism that pervades the film. Huston
wanted the story to "float somewhere in time,"
and everyone involved agreed that it couldn't be
either too slickly contemporary or too dated a
period piece. The solution required some imaginative compromises. For example, New York City
police cars were green until 1971 and blue and
white thereafter. If *Honor* was to avoid a specific
setting in time, which color should be used?
Washington decided to use old-model cars
painted in the newer colors.

He and set decorator Bruce Weintraub eventually hit upon 1962 as a frame of reference. "It
was a fun period, full of formica and plastic and
artificial flowers," Weintraub says. "It was the
Sixties, but before the 'Enlightenment.' Maerose
and Charley are about as far from Woodstock as
you can get."

Kathleen's character also had to suggest the
early 1960s without being specific. To play Irene,
she let her hair grow out from the blunt, no-
nonsense, chin-length bob she had worn as Joanna in *Crimes of Passion* (one critic had carped
that it made her look like a Berlin lesbian of the
1930s) to a softer, wavier, shoulder-length page-
boy. Some golden strands had appeared among
the chestnut locks in *Romancing* and had remained for *Crimes*. Now her hair was lightened
still further for the honey-blonde look that

knocks Charley out when he sees her among the dark-haired family members at a Prizzi wedding.

As the only outsider—a non-Prizzi and a Californian to boot—Kathleen was the only performer who was allowed to use her natural voice. The others learned to speak an exaggerated version of Sicilian Brooklynese: "We were supposed to sound like we were born in Sicily and never got across the East River," as one actor puts it. Huston hired actress and writer Julie Bovasso, who grew up in Brooklyn and is best known for her performance as John Travolta's mother in *Saturday Night Fever*, to coach everyone in the dialect he wanted for the Prizzis. The voice is used to best and most comic effect by Nicholson, who thickens it with a padded upper lip—no doubt an allusion to Brando's bulging lower lip in *The Godfather*. During the filming, Nicholson diligently used his Brooklyn accent constantly, off the set as well as on, to the mingled amusement and irritation of everyone else. The score by composer Alex North provided the musical equivalent of the accent, with clever adaptations of the operatic staples traditionally beloved of Mafia chieftains: Puccini, Rossini, Verdi. (The word *Mafia*, incidentally, doesn't appear in either Condon's book or the movie, although the identification of the Prizzi family with the Italian crime syndicate is obvious. Discussing *Prizzi's Honor* during an appearance on *Late Night with David Letterman*, Kathleen got a big laugh with the phrase, "There is no Mafia," which seems to have become the in joke of Huston's film crew.)

Kathleen's character, Irene, is in some ways a warmer, more offbeat version of *Body Heat*'s Matty Walker. In fact, a strange coincidence links the two characters: in both the book and the movie, "Irene Walker" confides to Charley on their first date that she's Polish and was born Maida Walcewicz. She claims she changed her name to Irene Walker to sound more American —but a more accurate Americanization of "Maida Walcewicz" would have been "Matty Walker." At any rate, Irene is as greedy, cynical, and coldblooded as Matty, but more sincere and fallible. Because the film has comedic elements, it allows her to show a playful, domestic side that was totally absent from the intense Matty. One of her best moments in the movie is when, after she and Charley collaborate on a kidnap-murder and he's preparing to haul the victim away in a van, she chirps a housewifely "See you at dinner, dear," and blows her bloody hubby a kiss.

Nicholson wasn't the only one to be confused by the strange mixture of humor and seriousness in *Honor*. What is one to make of a movie that combines scathing criticism of organized crime, police corruption, and amoral acquisitiveness with touches of sheer fun? Just when it seems as though the film has straightened up and is going to start taking itself seriously, Huston will insert a playful shot of toylike airplanes crisscrossing the stratosphere as Charley and Irene pursue their bicoastal affair. Or Charley will solemnly announce to Irene as a Mexican band strums away at an outdoor cafe, "This is gonna be our song," and ask, "What's it called, anyway?"

The love scenes between the two assassins (one critic called them "cobras with a nesting itch") were also playful, a fact which Kathleen appreciated—especially after *Crimes of Passion*. Huston and the screenplay called for an approach to romance that perfectly complements her own beliefs about cinematic sex. Of her scenes with Nicholson, she says, "The love scene on the bed was just a gas to do. I think that's one of the secrets of doing good sex on film, actually; I think that just having intense, intense kissing or touching is really kind of boring or archaic. I think the real joy is finding joy. I always try to laugh, always try to put in a gurgle of joy, because that touches people much more than watching someone pant. When we hit the headboard and it's banging the wall—there isn't a person in the world who doesn't know that sound!"

Prizzi's Honor is rich in deadpan lines, as when the devious Maerose justifies Irene's criminal proclivities by saying, "She's an American; she saw a chance to get ahead and she took it!"

Upon discovering that the woman he loves is involved in a scam that robbed the Prizzis of hundreds of thousands of dollars, Charley agonizes, "Do I ice her? Do I marry her?" And, reflecting on a hit that missed when a bodyguard failed to be distracted by a tossed doll, the lethal Irene sputters indignantly, "What kind of creep wouldn't catch a baby?"

The movie's labyrinthine plot demands close attention, a quality, unfortunately, that many viewers today are not willing to spare. Under the baroque twists and turns, however, is a simple story: boy meets girl, boy kills girl's husband and marries girl, family doesn't like girl, boy has to choose. But when the boy and girl are trained killers, a breakup is more than a divorce—the family urges Charley to kill Irene ("zotz" her, in the movie's idiom) and a disgruntled family member hires Irene to kill Charley. He has to kill the woman he loves to preserve the only life he's suited for, and she must either kill him or die. Their final confrontation, with Charley stretched out on Irene's silk sheets fingering the knife strapped to his leg under his pajamas and Irene babbling merrily in the dressing room as she stealthily readies her revolver, is the most suspenseful showdown since *High Noon.*

At the root of the story is the troubled, manipulative, wise Maerose Prizzi, Brooklyn's answer to Lucrezia Borgia. Brilliantly played by Anjelica Huston, she manages to manipulate all of the characters and events so that finally, in a touchingly radiant scene wryly set off by her nasal, "Holy cow, Charley," she gets what she has wanted all along—her man.

Kathleen, with her interest in characters who are themselves actors, enjoyed the ambiguities of her character's split personality: hit woman and happy homemaker. "It's a challenge to be nice, and then turn around and shoot somebody," she reported during the filming. She feels that Irene's motivations are similar to Matty Walker's: "Love isn't always the most important thing. At this moment, for Irene, survival is the most important thing."

Looking back now on the characters she's created, she says, "*Prizzi's Honor* reinforced the image of me as a manipulative woman, though I must say there are moments in *Prizzi* when my character is just this newlywed—she's got her job, but she's baking casseroles—that *I* like."

She also liked working with Nicholson, for whom she has nothing but praise. "I think he's a stunning actor," she says. "He's unique. Jack's great to work with. There's no hidden competitiveness. He's playing to me, not to Jack. He makes me feel warm and important. And Jack is technically excellent. You never have to worry if you are depending on a move or an emphasis or the pace of a line; you'll get it from Jack. I got a little spoiled working with him. All I had to do was act, that's all. I didn't have to take care of nobody else!"

Despite his relationship of many years with Anjelica Huston, Jack has a reputation as something of a ladies' man, and Kathleen admits, "It was a little rough flirtation-wise at first because he always pushes a little bit. When we were shooting in New York I asked him, 'So, are you having a good time?' and he said, 'How could I be having a good time? I'm working with a bunch of old men and a fucking *newlywed!*'" She adds with a laugh, "Actually, I think he and Anjelica probably had a very good time."

In fact, Kathleen claims that the whole *Prizzi's Honor* team was "really a happy family" and "had a ball, which always helps the on-screen performance. We still get together and have barbecues in New York." But while she loved working with Huston, whose polished manners and precise diction she admired, Kathleen may have benefited more from her good relationship with her leading man. Nicholson, she feels, is "a man's man," the sort of person who "would be an intensely loyal friend—if you were in a jam you could call for help and he'd always be there for you." Soon after making *Prizzi's Honor,* Kathleen would be helped by Nicholson's loyal friendship at a troubled point in her career.

But her difficulties were still in the future as

filming for *Honor* wrapped at the end of 1984. When the film was released in the early summer of 1985, Huston's stature in the film world and his masterful handling of an unusual story guaranteed it plenty of attention. *Variety* and *MacLean's* were dubious about *Prizzi's Honor*, feeling that the blend of comedy and seriousness didn't quite come off. *Variety* pointed out that the film's early publicity played up its comic aspects and conjectured that some viewers would be dismayed by its dark tone, complex plot, and grim conclusion.

The rest of the critics and reviewers, however, leaped happily onto the Prizzi bandwagon and applauded a director who dared to offer something more challenging than teen-oriented masturbation fantasies and predictable action flicks. The favorable notices poured in—for Huston, for Nicholson, and for Kathleen as the upwardly mobile Irene, drily described by Richard Schickel as "pioneering an occupation previously closed to her sex." Some writers, while conceding her beauty and style, felt that she lacked depth because her character is really Charley's fantasy, a glamorous outsider who never achieves the three-dimensional reality of the Prizzis. But her suppleness, smoothness, and versatility were praised, and Pauline Kael asserted that if she seemed pallid, the fault lay in the character and not in Kathleen's performance.

Only one reviewer leveled his guns at Kathleen in earnest. Writing in *Mademoiselle* magazine, Ron Rosenbaum titled his review "The Curse of a Pretty Face" and pointlessly took issue, not with Kathleen's talent or lack of it, but with her looks. "Here's an actress who's definitely Too Pretty for her own good," he claimed. "However torn she is with conflicting passions, there's still a prom-queen, vanilla-ice-cream prettiness that undermines any depth of character she's trying to create." Fortunately Rosenbaum's cranky opinion—had he seen *Crimes of Passion*?—was a minority of one. At the other end of the spectrum, *People* called Kathleen "glorious, the sexiest presence in movies right now and a prodigious actress to boot."

Although *Prizzi's Honor* won the New York Film Critics' award for Best Picture of 1985, Kathleen won no awards for her creation of Irene. *Prizzi's Honor* was neither a mainstream box-office success like *Romancing the Stone* nor a virtuoso demonstration of sheer acting ability like *Crimes of Passion*. But it gave her the chance to work with two masters of her craft and added a prestigious credit to her growing list of accomplishments. Beyond a doubt, Kathleen Turner was now solidly established, no flash in the movie camera's pan. Soon after finishing *Honor*, she said, "The first time I felt successful was just this past year. I finally became free from the anxiety of 'Do they want me?' "

She added, "I think success is great. I meet people who feel guilty or are apologetic about it, but that doesn't make sense, because everything you work for is aimed toward that. Of course, for an actor, success is never a given. After you prove yourself in one part, you go on to another. You're constantly proving yourself." The uproar that arose over Kathleen's next picture proved that she could speak up for her aesthetic principles at the risk of jeopardizing her career.

8

Riled on the Nile

When *Romancing the Stone* aired on cable television during the summer of 1985, it was followed by Michael Douglas announcing, "Watch for the further adventures of Jack and Joan in *The Jewel of the Nile,* coming this Christmas." To many fans of *Romancing,* this was the first news of a sequel. Other viewers, though, had been following the sensational tabloid accounts of a $25 million lawsuit against Kathleen by Twentieth Century-Fox, who claimed that she had refused to honor her contractual obligation to appear in a second Joan Wilder adventure.

The claims and counterclaims of the suit are complex and contradictory, as might be expected when Kathleen is involved. The behind-the-scenes story sheds considerable light on the practices of those who make big movies for big money.

Although many people think that a movie sequel is made as a result of popular demand, studios and producers are in fact pretty good at guessing the sequel power of a film even before the first installment opens. That's why, when Kathleen signed up in May of 1983 to appear in *Romancing the Stone* for Twentieth Century-Fox, her contract included an agreement to appear in one more movie for Fox, a sequel called *The Jewel of the Nile*.

Douglas, *Romancing*'s producer, makes his decision to produce a sequel sound like a creative process: "At first, I was reluctant to do a sequel. But so many people came up to me and asked what I thought happened to the characters. It got me thinking and I decided, yeah, it would be interesting to find out what happened to them. It's so unusual to have a movie like *Romancing*, an action-adventure, and have people interested in what happens to the characters." In reality, however, Fox proposed making the sequel almost as soon as *Romancing* opened, and their decision had less to do with creative speculation than with rip-roaring box-office receipts. Douglas agreed to proceed, and then Fox dropped the bombshell: the film must be ready to open by Christmas of 1985. Douglas admits to being a little shell-shocked.

"Every picture I'd ever been involved with had been a labor of love, something I'd struggled with for four or five years," he says. "And all of a sudden I had studios asking me to deliver a picture, from the germ of an idea to a finished print, in fourteen months.'' Of course, he had more than just the germ of an idea; he had the film's main characters, Jack Colton and Joan Wilder, and he had its starting point, the shot of the happy couple sailing away into the sunset. But he didn't have a screenplay.

Douglas claims that he didn't ask Diane Thomas to write *Jewel* because she was under contract to develop three pictures for Steven Spielberg's company, Amblin Entertainment, although he was apparently able to rope her in as a troubleshooter later in the project. Instead he assigned the team of Mark Rosenthal and Lawrence Konner, who had written *The Legend of Billie Jean,* to come up with a script for *Jewel.* By November of 1985 they had completed the first draft. It was submitted to the actors, including Kathleen, and that's when Douglas's *real* troubles started.

Kathleen asked Fox to let her make *The Money Pit,* produced by Steven Spielberg and directed by Richard Benjamin, before working on *Jewel;* if they had agreed, of course, *Jewel* would have missed its targeted release date. When the studio refused, Kathleen announced that she found the script unacceptable and couldn't appear in the film as it stood. In a surprisingly quick and severe response, Fox attorney Bertram Fields entered a lawsuit against Kathleen in Los

Angeles Superior Court on February 4, 1985, charging her with breach of contract.

Fox claimed that on January 22, Kathleen had demanded what was termed "a vastly increased sum of money" before appearing in *Jewel*. According to Fox, Kathleen wasn't entitled to a pay increase; the studio also asked for an injunction to prevent her from working on any other movies until *Jewel* was completed. The sum Fox demanded if Kathleen did not make *Jewel* was enormous—$20 million in lost profits and $5 million in punitive damages.

Kathleen's attorney, Larry Stein, told the press: "Kathleen had asked Fox to let her make the Spielberg film before doing the sequel. But Fox didn't want to make any accommodation for her at all. Kathleen's problems with the sequel all concern serious creative differences and we were simply also discussing compensation for her having to deal with those differences. But Fox's suit makes it appear that money was a key issue. It wasn't. I don't know why they sued so impetuously while still in the talking stage. Maybe they're just trying to intimidate her."

The suit was a shocking surprise to Kathleen, who had no idea Fox would take her to court. She first heard the news when she walked into her apartment building that evening and the doorman said, "Oh, twenty-five million dollars?" and showed her the *New York Post*, with a screaming headline about the lawsuit. "I was absolutely crazy," she recalls. "And I never said I wouldn't do the movie! I just didn't want to do a bad one, and I wanted to address the money issue up front."

The much-vaunted "chemistry" Kathleen and Douglas had shown in *Romancing* now turned explosive. One movie industry insider close to Douglas reports that he expressed great bitterness toward Kathleen, claiming that she owed him the sequel because *Romancing* had made her a star. Kathleen admits that *Romancing* was her first popular success and gave her great visibility, but adds, "I did a good job. I think I owe Michael for the opportunity and his judgment and vision, but I don't owe anyone for the work I do. That makes me furious."

Communication between the two collapsed entirely until, as Kathleen says, "Jack Nicholson sort of interceded and got me and Michael talking again." Douglas promised a script rewrite, the offer to do *The Money Pit* was withdrawn (the role went to Shelley Long), and the lawsuit was dropped. "There never was any need to go to any kind of lawsuit," Kathleen now says. "I should have known enough about Michael to know he'd have things fixed by the time we were ready to shoot it."

As it was eventually filmed, *Jewel* takes up the story of Jack and Joan six months after they sailed

down West End Avenue and attempts to answer
the question: Can a romance writer and a foot-
loose adventurer live happily ever after? The answer at first appears to be "no." Douglas explains
that *Romancing* was about falling in love, but *Jewel*
is about making a commitment to a relationship
(the trendy film topic of the mid-1980s). "*Romancing* was Joan's story," he says. "In the sequel
we tried to show how the feelings Jack and Joan
developed for each other in the first movie
weather the trials and tribulations of real life."

Some real life. The story opens on the
French Riviera, where Joan's nagging discontent
with their free-wheeling shipboard lifestyle is
making it hard for her to complete her latest sac-
charine saga. Hers is the dilemma of the romantic
who has begun to become disillusioned with romance. She throws her typewriter into the sea
and cries, "Exotic ports, great parties, spectacu-
lar sunsets—it's not enough!" She and Jack
argue, and she is persuaded by a suave Arab po-
tentate named Omar (played by Greek actor
Spiros Focas) to stop writing trash and start writing serious literature—namely, his biography. He
lures her to his remote desert fastness, where she
abruptly discovers to her dismay that he wanted
her for her trash all along. He expects her to
churn out a gushy, flattering portrait of him as he
prepares to seize power in his nameless country,

with the aid of a mysterious something called "the Jewel of the Nile."

Joan tries to escape and, in doing so, meets "the Jewel," a tribal wise man loonily portrayed by Avner Eisenberg. Meanwhile, Jack and Ralph, Jack's stubby sparring partner from *Romancing*, played by Danny DeVito, show up at Omar's fortress. Is Jack looking for Joan, looking for "the Jewel" (which he believes is of the mineral variety), or a little of both? Will Ralph turn traitor or turn out to be true blue? Will the band of wandering, juggling Sufi mystics (portrayed by the five-member Flying Karamazov Brothers) get "the Jewel" to the holy city in time to stop Omar's takeover? Will Jack and Joan escape from the torture chamber—and, if they do, will torture convince Jack to settle down and get married? The answers are just a camel ride and a train chase away.

The "creative differences" alluded to by Kathleen's attorney centered around Rosenthal and Konner's script, which Kathleen felt lacked "the spirit and fun" of the *Romancing* and turned Joan into "a real wimp." Although she liked the topical subject—an attempted political coup in an Arab nation—she felt that the script suffered from having been written by men instead of by a woman. "I like Joan Wilder," she explains. "She was my first sympathetic character, and I was anxious that the sequel be the same quality as the original." Joan's character and strength were undermined by the first draft of *Jewel:* "She committed no actions to save herself, and she had nothing to do with the woman you saw at the end of *Romancing.*"

The script problems most often cited by Kathleen, however, concerned what she calls "questionable taste in scenes such as the one where a bunch of Nubian pygmies tells Jack, 'If you give us the woman for an hour, we'll let you live.'" Referring to a scene in which a bunch of Africans drag Joan into a hut, she claims, "I don't like rape jokes."

A purist might wonder whether this feminist fervor wasn't a bit self-serving. After all, Kathleen apparently didn't balk at the one truly gratuitous bit of tasteless humor in *Romancing,* when Joan's elderly neighbor expresses a fear of being raped in an elevator. And, although Diane Thomas was brought in to revise the *Jewel* script and quell Kathleen's qualms, she didn't eliminate a long sequence in which Jack fights a burly tribesman with Joan as the jackpot. No doubt some changes were made, but Kathleen may have decided that, having taken a stand, she could now afford to back down a bit.

Rape jokes and creative conflicts aside, Kathleen frankly acknowledges that money was part of the problem. She was entitled to a share of *Romancing*'s earnings, and the studio told her that the film was somewhere between seven and three million dollars in the hole. "Here's a film that's the fourth highest selling cassette in the country," she says scornfully. "It did something like $78 million in domestic business and $30 million overseas." She adds a remark that can be construed either as another statement of high feminist principles or a straightforward case of resentment that Douglas's take from the film was larger than hers: "I suppose what infuriated me was how much less women are paid in Hollywood than men." With someone simultaneously as independent and as driven as Kathleen, both meanings probably apply.

Once the lawsuit was dropped—only three weeks after it was filed—work began on the $17.5-million *Jewel of the Nile*. In addition to the endless tinkering with the script, Douglas faced massive personnel and logistics problems that had to be solved before shooting could begin on schedule in North Africa in April. Because he was starring in Sir Richard Attenborough's film version of *A Chorus Line*, being shot in New York, he set up his *Jewel* production crew by long-distance telephone, making calls from his dressing room between takes.

He soon discovered that he had taken on a gigantic headache. "*Romancing* was basically Kathleen, Danny, me and a few other people running around in Mexico," he says. But *Jewel* involved five locations (four in Morocco and one in Nice, France), 130 vehicles that had to be shipped to Morocco, a crew of 300 people speaking sixteen languages, and a private fleet of three planes to airlift people and supplies between locations in the desert.

Robert Zemeckis, who had directed *Romancing*, was unavailable. He was directing a Steven Spielberg production called *Back to the Future*, which ended up being the top-grossing film of 1985. Douglas turned to Lewis Teague, who had attracted a cult following when he made Roger Corman's gangster classic, *The Lady in Red*, for half a million dollars. Since then, Teague had demonstrated his flair for humor (*Alligator*), action (*Cujo*), and special effects (*Cat's Eye*). He immediately agreed to direct *Jewel*—"I couldn't hesitate," he says. "There wasn't time"—and claims he had second thoughts only when he looked at the script, looked at the schedule, and arrived in Morocco.

A North African desert location had sounded perfect to Douglas and Kathleen after the mud and rain of Mexico. They were looking forward to warmth and sand, but what they found was worse than the jungle.

Things weren't so bad in Fez, where the scenes in Omar's palace and the train sequences were filmed. The first problems were political and administrative. As if Kathleen's critical scrutiny hadn't been enough, the script was submitted to a state censor who had to verify that the film contained no anti-Islamic elements. Douglas instructed the writers to place the action in a fictional country, and they tried to avoid making Omar look *too* much like Libya's fanatical Moammar Qaddafi, who happens to be an ally of Morocco's King Hassan II.

Douglas and *Romancing* had taken a few lumps from Colombians and others who complained that the film made all Latin Americans look like thugs or greaseballs. He expected a similar perception by the Arabs. "We have good Arabs and bad Arabs in the film, but as we aren't doing a character study, mostly we've used broad strokes," he said at one point, explaining why some of those "broad strokes" might look like stereotypes. "Perhaps the Arabs won't like what we've done. It's only natural for them to be sensitive. But we don't cater to private interests. Americans are used to criticism. *Deliverance* didn't have good things to say about rednecks, or *China Syndrome* about big business. But if a picture works, those elements are not offensive."

Whatever the Arabs' feelings about the way they're portrayed in *Jewel,* plenty of them turned up as extras in the crowd scenes—for $2 a day, a respectable wage in their poverty-stricken country. But only one of Teague's second assistants and the official representative of Morocco's government spoke Arabic.

The government's cooperation was especially important when it came to getting movie gear through customs. Production designer Terence Knight complained that everything, "right down to bags of nuts and bolts," was held up, but the trickiest negotiations involved crates of weaponry, including Uzi machine guns from Morocco's enemy Israel. As Morocco was a country at war (with guerilla rebels in the south), even prop weapons couldn't cross the borders without the special permission of the king.

If the Uzis were tough, the fighter plane was well-nigh impossible. Douglas's brother Joel, who coproduced *Jewel,* says the full-scale replica of an American F-16 jet that demolishes Omar's home town without ever leaving the ground is so accurate that only a detailed examination by an expert would reveal it as a fake. It took a team of British experts four months to build the $200,000 prop, which was capable of firing real rockets, and the crew wondered what the outcome would be if a Soviet satellite spotted the jet just a few minutes from the border of Algeria, Morocco's hostile neighbor.

They didn't ignite World War III, but they had plenty of lesser headaches. Morocco has no film labs, so each day's work was rushed to London to be processed and then back to Morocco for review by Douglas and Teague. The villa that housed the cast when they moved to Ouarzarzate to film the desert scenes had no plumbing. The desert was hotter than anyone had expected, much hotter.

Recalls DeVito, "You ever try to walk across a small patch of sand at the beach when it's 95 degrees? Burns, doesn't it? Well, out on the Sahara it was 130 degrees. Your underwear was filled with sand. You're sweating like crazy. Your camel has the worst breath in the world. You can't wait for someone to say 'Action!' so you can start walking and feel the air move across your face." Like Kathleen, Douglas, and other cast members, DeVito had to learn to ride a camel, and eventually he developed a relationship based on mutual respect with a beast named Humphrey. As for the rest of the stunts, he says modestly, "I don't think it takes much special skill to be strung up by your foot or thrown in a sand dune. I experienced all those things growing up in New Jersey."

Ironically, in view of everyone's relief that there would be no tropical rainstorms in *this* picture, freak rains broke up the shooting schedule. After Knight had spent seven weeks building a set in the desert—castle walls, bridges, and nearly two miles of road—a six-year drought was broken. It rained for eight days, a local record; "If it had happened 2,000 years ago, it would have gotten into the Bible," Knight says. An eight-foot wall of water rushed down from the mountains and destroyed the set in fifteen seconds. It had to be entirely rebuilt. As if Knight didn't have enough problems, he found that the 14,000-square-foot Royal Square of the city of Meknes, where the huge crowd scene at the film's climax was filmed, is regarded as an antique. He had to stage the entire scene—thousands of crew members, cast members, extras, and animals—so that nobody so much as touched one of the walls.

As he had done after the filming of *Romancing,* Douglas praised Kathleen's high spirits. Some of the filming had been scheduled to take place during Ramadan, the Islamic holy month when no one is permitted to eat, drink, work, or even have sex during the day, and everyone celebrates when the sun goes down. (One climactic scene, involving 2,500 extras, had to be shot precisely at twilight during the first week of Ramadan. No one on the production staff knew anything about Islamic customs—they were dubbed "the Jews of the Nile" by studio executives—and nobody had any idea what would happen if the signal to eat occurred while the scene was being shot.) Because of Ramadan, many scenes were shot after sunset, and "at night all the bugs came out," Douglas says, "huge great beasts, and Kathleen never squealed. We were also confronted with strange local customs, tribal suspicion, and so on. Jesus!"

Kathleen did many of her own stunts—the close camera coverage wouldn't permit the use of doubles in some scenes, even if she had wanted to use one. For the scene in Omar's torture chamber, she and Douglas spent the better part of four days strung up by their wrists over a pit. She studied fencing for one sequence and dangled from the side of a speeding train for another. "I was well tied off," she says. "If I lost my grip, I wouldn't fall and be crushed. But still, you know, you go home at night and wonder, 'Does everybody do this?' "

She found the location work wonderfully colorful and exciting, but admits that she felt a little claustrophobic at times. "A single woman simply could not go out alone—partly out of respect to the local fundamentalist Islamic culture, and partly for fear of being stoned," she says, referring to the fate that sometimes overtakes women who go out of doors without a veil and a man in Arab countries. Her claustrophobia was periodically relieved by visits from Jay, who flew to Morocco every three weeks.

Douglas had wisely scheduled the scenes in Nice, which opened the movie, to be shot last. After months in the desert, the cast and crew were delighted with the beach, the cool waters of the Mediterranean, and the wonderful French food in the commissary at La Victorine Studios. One of the last scenes to be filmed was the autograph party for Joan; film buffs may be interested to learn that it took place in the roof garden of the Cannes Film Festival building.

Despite bureaucratic and meteorological obstacles, the shooting of *Jewel* finished only ten days behind schedule, on July 23. Cast and crew members dispersed, and Douglas and Teague began the grueling postproduction tasks of editing, creating the sound track, and so on. They agreed to dedicate the film to three members of the crew who had died in a plane crash while scouting for locations: production designer Richard Dawking, location manager Brian Coates, and pilot Richard Kotch. Sadly, they had to add a fourth name to the movie's dedication. On October 21, Diane Thomas was killed in Los Angeles. She had been a passenger in a car driven by her boyfriend, actor Stephen Norman, who skidded out of control in light rain on the twisting Pacific Coast Highway. Thomas was pronounced dead on the scene, another passenger died later, and police announced that Norman, who had been drinking, would be charged with vehicular manslaughter.

The Jewel of the Nile lived up to Fox's terms and reached the nation's theaters in time for Christmas 1985. But its reception was somewhat disappointing.

Most reviewers panned the screenplay; it seemed that they agreed with Kathleen that it lacked the sparkle and wit of Thomas's *Romancing*. There were some wonderful moments, such as Joan's publisher's description of Jack ("His favorite author is the guy who wrote 'Pull tab to open' ") and Jack's outburst when he and Joan are slung over the pit in Omar's dungeon by ropes that are being gnawed by rats *and* corroded by acid. "What sick, twisted mind would even think up something as disgusting as this?" he raves, to which Joan sheepishly replies, "Mine" and confesses she cooked up the torture scheme for one of her books.

On the whole, though *Newsweek* and *New York* liked the sequel better than its predecessor, critics felt that *Jewel* suffered from what *Playboy*'s Bruce Williamson calls "the law of diminishing returns in moviemaking." Audiences seemed to agree. *Jewel* took in a whopping $28 million in its first month and another $30 million in the following three months, but its momentum slowed in spite of a vigorous ad campaign and plenty of media hype. It is unlikely that its earnings will equal those of *Romancing the Stone*.

Prospects for a third Jack-and-Joan adventure appear dim, although Kathleen says that quite a few fans have asked whether she'll make one. "I'm not intrigued by the idea now," she says. "I'm not sure she's that interesting to ex-

plore anymore." But she adds, perhaps feeling
that she has dismissed her most popular and re-
munerative character a little too cavalierly, "In a
couple of years, people may still want to see Jack
and Joan. If I go too far and disillusion people or
lose touch—because I think that's bound to happen; you can't keep the same audience appeal if
you want to do things that interest you—then I
could do Joan again. Maybe Joan Wilder is a net."

One unusual media spin-off brought Kathleen to an unexpected audience of rock fans: *Jewel*
made it onto MTV. In November of 1985, Kathleen, Douglas, and DeVito convened at the Academy Theatre in London to tape a rock video to
the *Jewel*'s theme song, "When the Going Gets
Tough, the Tough Get Going," by Billy Ocean.
In the video, clips from the film are spliced into
footage of Ocean singing while the three actors,
calling themselves the Jewelettes and done up in
white tuxedos, mimic the smooth background
moves of soul groups like the Temptations—
DeVito even gets to imitate Clarence Clemons
with a saxophone. They aren't just lip-synching,
either, but crooning away under cover of the recorded soundtrack. Douglas says, "We were singing our asses off. You begin to believe in yourself,
until they turn the sound off and you're there
croaking."

Cast members plugged the movie and the
video on talk shows and in newspapers. Kathleen

took a clip from the video to the Letterman show, where the host poked fun at it, saying, "It's misleading. I know for a fact that nowhere in the movie do you and Billy Ocean dress up in white suits and sing together. What happened to the *Prizzi's Honor* video?"

But if Kathleen was disturbed by the less than wildly enthusiastic reception *The Jewel of the Nile* received, she didn't have time to show it. Ever since February of 1985, when she was bogged down in her lawsuit with Fox and her script disputes with Douglas, she had been angling for her next role. By the time *Jewel* was being reviewed, she had not only completed another picture but was also busy with Jay making big plans for her personal life.

9

Airport XVII

Kathleen and Jay Weiss were married in August of 1984, less than a year after they had met. The wedding took place during the brief lull between the filming of *Crimes of Passion* and that of *Prizzi's Honor*.

By that time, of course, Kathleen had become quite well known. Her *Body Heat*, *Man with Two Brains*, and *Crimes of Passion* characters outweighed the likable Joan Wilder of *Romancing* in the public eye, and her early image of mystery, glamour, and bitchiness had clung to her like Matty Walker's skin-tight skirts. Kathleen recalls that when Jay went back to his home town shortly before their marriage, the first question everyone asked was, "Is she really a bitch?" She says with a laugh, "We have a pact: When someone asks, 'What's she really like?' I'll always love him for saying, 'She makes great fried chicken.' "

Despite the instant rapport that Kathleen claims she and Jay felt, they are from wildly different backgrounds. Kathleen, born in Missouri and raised all over the world, is as WASP-y as they come; Jay is, as she describes him, "a nice Jewish boy." They were married in a Jewish ceremony by a Reform rabbi. The Turner family even wore yarmulkas.

Jay moved into Kathleen's Chelsea apartment and began looking for a larger place. Meanwhile Kathleen began work on *Prizzi's Honor*. Most of the film was shot in New York, so the newlyweds weren't separated. During the filming of the Los Angeles segments—the last ones to be shot—Jay visited the West Coast with Kathleen. Then, in January of 1985, just as the furor over the *Jewel of the Nile* script began to brew, Jay bought a five-story, balconied townhouse on West 10th Street in Greenwich Village. It is a historic building, designed by nineteenth-century architect James Renwick, who also designed St. Patrick's Cathedral, Grace Church, and other New York landmarks. Jay Weiss's ownership added a troubled chapter to its history.

He and Kathleen planned to live in the building's two-story garden apartment, which was vacant when Jay bought it. But during the spring of 1985, while Kathleen was embroiled first in the *Jewel* dispute and then in the start of filming, Jay found himself in trouble with the building's other seven tenants, who complained about Jay's extensive renovations to the garden apartment. According to the tenants, the clouds of plaster dust raised by the work penetrated the entire building. On top of the dust, they were also inconvenienced by the relining of the chimney from the Weiss apartment, which made it necessary to break holes in the wall on each floor. One annoyed tenant even tried to confront Kathleen and Jay soon after they moved into the building, as they were rushing out to a waiting stretch limousine to be taken to a performance of the Martha Graham Dance Company at Lincoln Center. Jay had given each tenant $100 in compensation for the dust and annoyance, but apparently they felt that it wasn't enough.

Jay maintained that the problems were exaggerated by the complainers' ringleader, a rent-controlled tenant who, says Jay, wanted to be paid $50,000 to move out of the building. No doubt Jay would have liked to see the last of this difficult neighbor, but he was obliged to turn the offer down because he didn't have the money. "I'm not John Zaccaro, unfortunately," he remarked, in a wry reference to the real-estate scandals that plagued the husband of vice-presidential candidate Geraldine Ferraro. He also had trouble with another tenant: John Ehrlichman of the Watergate crowd, who was living in New Mexico and had sublet his apartment, was angry when Jay tried to get rid of the subtenant. All in all, their move into the 10th Street building wasn't exactly a happy homecoming for Kathleen and Jay.

As if the problems in their own building weren't a sufficient headache for any landlord, during the summer Jay became one of the targets of an investigation by the office of the Attorney General of New York into alleged real-estate fraud. The purpose of the investigation was to determine whether illegal subleases had been used to raise rents higher than the level allowed under rent stabilization in five buildings between West 35th Street and East 94th Street in Manhattan. The companies who own the buildings are involved with two firms owned by Jay and his sister, Laurie—Troy Ventures and J.L. Madison Properties. The investigation promised to be a long-drawn-out and complicated matter, although a spokeswoman for the office of Attorney General Robert Abrams says, "We have not subpoenaed Jay Weiss," and adds that there is no reason to assume that he is involved in any wrongdoing.

The investigation may have slowed Jay's other real-estate and entrepreneurial activities, but it didn't stop them. He and a partner, Morris Jaffe (who was also named in the subpoenas issued by the Attorney General), recently bought the popular Danceteria nightclub on West 21st Street.

While Jay was coping with these distractions,

he was also making periodic dashes to Morocco to visit Kathleen on the set of *Jewel*. The completion of filming, however, did not signal her return to the New York duplex. When *Jewel* wrapped on the French Riviera in late July, Kathleen had less than one week in which to relax before reporting to the rolling wine country of northern California for her next movie assignment, *Peggy Sue Got Married*.

She had been angling for the lead part in *Peggy Sue*, directed by Francis Coppola (director of *The Godfather* and *Apocalypse Now*) since the beginning of the year. The role—a forty-two-year-old woman who relives her eighteenth year with her adult memories intact after the breakup of her marriage—had originally gone to Debra Winger. A back injury caused Winger to bow out, and the search was on for a replacement. In February, while she was under fire from Twentieth Century-Fox over *Jewel*, Kathleen had met with Coppola. David Guc felt that it was unlikely that Kathleen would get the part, in view of her highly publicized problems with Fox and the fact that she would almost certainly have to do *Jewel* before appearing in any other film. But Coppola was apparently sufficiently impressed with Kathleen's potential for the role that he was willing to wait until she became available. Before *Jewel* was completed, he announced that she would star in

Peggy Sue, to be produced by Tri-Star Productions.

It is easy to see the attraction of a film like *Peggy Sue Got Married* for a performer like Kathleen. For one thing, it offered the opportunity to work with one of the most highly regarded directors in the world, a man with several monumental successes to his credit, and some daring failures as well, such as the disastrous *One from the Heart.* For another, it had what Kathleen is always looking for: a new acting challenge. None of her earlier films had explored the subject of age or required her to act older or younger than she was. Now, in one film, she would be forced to be significantly older *and* younger than her real age (an interesting variation on Kathleen's favorite theme of characters who are themselves playing more than one part or showing more than one personality). Another attraction—especially on the heels of the *Jewel* fiasco—was the script, which she felt was well written and substantial.

As far as the subject matter of the film is concerned, Kathleen feels little affinity with it. *Peggy Sue* opens at a high-school reunion and, says Kathleen—whose high-school years certainly did not follow the conventional all-American pattern eulogized by Bruce Springsteen in the song "Glory Days"—"The only good memories I have of high school are of this theater group I was in. I can't imagine going back to high school." She adds, "Peggy Sue was a cheerleader in high school. Cheerleaders were a joke in London, where I went to high school. We formed a cheerleading squad for the teachers, who played the high-school basketball team, which was called the Eagles. The teachers were the Bald Eagles, and we cheered for them. We went out and spreadeagled between shots."

Her lack of nostalgia for her high-school years didn't keep Kathleen from putting in a highly professional performance. As always, she used physical cues such as movement and style of walking to express her character. One interviewer who was present on the set during a scene in which Kathleen was made up to look older reports that her posture and her very walk altered to portray an older, sadder woman; Coppola, viewing a close-up of the scene on a small camera monitor on his lap, shook his head in admiration and said, "This is great stuff." *Peggy Sue Got Married* was released in late 1986. Like her two Joan Wilder films, it may deal a blow to her femme fatale image and showcase her girl-next-door qualities. It is certainly another step away from the thing she dreads most of all: typecasting.

Kathleen took a break from the *Peggy Sue* filming to return to Springfield in October to receive an award from Southwest Missouri State as its "outstanding young alumna" of the year. The college had apparently decided to claim the now-famous Kathleen as one of its own in spite of the fact that she had left SMSC without graduating. No doubt Kathleen relished the irony of receiving such an honor from a school where she felt so unhappy and limited that she left after her junior year. Recalling the event several months later on *Late Night with David Letterman*, she described the award as a crystal pyramid and said that when she brought it back to her mother's house, her grandfather had looked at it and testily remarked, "What good is it? You can't drink out of it!"

Kathleen's grandfather appears to be something of a character. When she took Jay to Missouri to meet the family for the first time, her grandfather challenged Kathleen to a bourbon-drinking contest straight out of *Raiders of the Lost Ark*. "He said he could drink me under the table," Kathleen says. "I even caught him cheating, filling up my glass when I wasn't looking." Like the Karen Allen character in *Raiders*, though, Kathleen hung in there and outlasted the old man.

Her relationship with everyone in her family remains close. She makes a point of inviting her sister or one of her brothers to visit her on the set of every film she appears in, so that her siblings will feel involved in her career. And, ever since her father died, she has had a special kinship with her mother. "We went through such a similar period," she says, speaking of their sorrowful and confused return to the United States after Richard Turner's death. "As I was starting college, we were both looking for a job, friends, a place to live. I think it created a closeness that I wouldn't otherwise have had with her." The whole family meets at Mrs. Turner's to celebrate Christmas each year, and Kathleen says she still enjoys visiting the "absolutely beautiful" Missouri countryside, especially the Ozark Mountains.

Those Turner family gatherings will probably be larger in the years to come. Kathleen and Jay have said repeatedly that they plan to start a family soon. When the children arrive, they can expect to become familiar with stage sets and dressing rooms on both coasts; reminded of the excitement of her own globe-trotting childhood, Kathleen says firmly, "I certainly intend to drag *my* kids everywhere."

Not surprisingly, such announcements are often followed by rumors that Kathleen is pregnant. She is small boned and has a hearty appetite (she surprised one interviewer, who was used to "Perrier and fruit salad types," by ordering nachos, burritos with extra beans, and two Dos Equis beers at a luncheon meeting at the Black Rock cafe in the Village). Unlike many celebrities today, she doesn't sing the praises of her exercise routine or boast about her private workout coach. Indeed, she says, she does a "California workout, where you put on a jogging suit and then have a martini." Irene, of *Prizzi's Honor,* is fuller-faced and less slender than Matty of *Body Heat* or Dolores of *Brains,* and the Joan Wilder of *Jewel* seems a shade larger than the Joan of *Romancing.* These days, Kathleen's figure—revealed in a *Playboy* foldout in the May 1986 issue, which shows her wearing nothing but a diaphanous pink nightgown—is soft and rounded, resembling a somewhat less buxom Marilyn Monroe more than it does the wiry, muscular look typical of most models and actresses in the 1980s.

Because her weight does appear to fluctuate easily, some of Kathleen's public appearances have given rise to speculations about pregnancy. In May of 1986, for example, when she flew to St. Louis, Missouri, to join hands with her mother and thousands of other volunteers in Hands Across America, she was photographed by *People* with curly, light-blonde hair cut in bangs (perhaps for the part of Peggy Sue) and a distinctly plumper although still dimpled face. But neither she nor Jay has indicated that she is expecting a baby.

Nor has Kathleen announced her next film project, now that *Peggy Sue* is in the can. Instead she is contemplating a return to the New York stage in *The Widow's Blind Date,* a play by Israel Horovitz that premiered in Gloucester, Massachusetts, and has played in Boston, Los Angeles, and France. The plot has some similarities to that of *Peggy Sue,* although its subject matter is much bleaker: a woman who was gang-raped in high school returns to her home town years later and finds that two of the men who took part in the rape haven't changed. The woman and the two men are the only characters in the play. If the male roles can be cast and producers found, Kathleen may appear on or off Broadway sometime in late 1986 or early 1987. She says she is looking forward to a stage production because "you don't have to subvert the power of your work to technical things," and explains, "In movies, the camera is more important than you. It wears you down when you do an intense scene and the director says, 'Let's do it again, honey, there was a hair caught in the gate of the projector.' "

Neither stage work nor her plans for a family, however, is likely to sidetrack Kathleen Turner's film career for long. After only eight movies (one of them never released) in just five years, she has become a major power in the entertainment industry. As one Hollywood executive says, "*Everyone*—stars and directors—wants to work with Turner. There are bigger box-office names, but not for long." She has undoubtedly proven her talent and her ability to appeal to a huge audience. But intelligence and independence have created some problems for her. One studio executive conceded her intelligence, saying, "She has an I.Q. like a professional bowling score," but he didn't necessarily mean it as a compliment. She feels that she is less "submissive" than some people in the film industry like their actresses to be, and she adds, "I do have some difficulty playing dumb, and in this business that limits you."

In addition, while she admits she has learned something from every movie she's made and everyone she's worked with, Kathleen feels she is ready to make more decisions where her projects are concerned. She liked being involved with the production details of lighting and blocking in *Body Heat* and *Prizzi's Honor,* and she would like to have more to do with such matters in the future. The disaster of the original *Jewel* script showed that she has strong ideas about her characters and their integrity and that she's willing to scrap with studio executives, if necessary, to make a point. (Although she may be the most notorious, due to the $25-million lawsuit, Kathleen's not the only actress on the Hollywood scene these days to express her opinions to the dismay of studio management; within the past few years, Jessica Lange argued with the director of *Frances* about the lack of order on the set and Glenn Close fought furiously with the cinematographer of *Jagged Edge* over camera angles that she considered unflattering.)

Because Kathleen clearly wants to have more control over the projects she's involved in, she has decided that the next step in her film career will be a production company of her own. She is working on plans for such a company and hopes to put together a team to review scripts and select promising projects for development.

Although she conscientiously avoids what she calls "message movies," in which the character is less important than the theme, Kathleen is increasingly active on behalf of several organizations with whose goals she agrees. One is Planned Parenthood; she serves on its Board of Advisors. While she would be "horrified to have to make a decision about an abortion," she supports the mother's right to choose, saying, "It is more appalling to me to bring these children into the world without any resources, without any choice, without love and a future."

She has also appeared at benefits in support of Norman Lear's group, People for the American Way, which battles censorship, always a pertinent concern to members of the entertainment industry and perhaps more so to Kathleen after the attacks that were made on *Crimes of Passion*. "I find that a lot of these born-again-Christian Falwell characters—Falwell in particular—are absolutely frightening, because they are making political judgments under the blanket of Christian sanctity," she told *Playboy* interviewer David

Sheff. "I definitely think they're a serious threat to our country."

Kathleen is well aware of the boost that a celebrity's support can give to a cause. While she feels that fame entails a great deal of responsibility, she also believes that celebrity-worship is carried to an extreme in America, where—she cites a recent survey—"more people know who Madonna is than know who the Secretary of State is." With her pragmatic approach to life, her tendency to speak her mind no matter how acerbic her opinions, and her lack of veneration for the trappings of fame, she is unlikely to be swept off balance, no matter how high she rises in the future.

After *Prizzi's Honor*, Jack Nicholson advised Kathleen to "sit back and let her price go up." Her price may be going up, but Kathleen will probably not sit back for long. She finds it impossible to imagine not working, even after she has children, and describes herself as "very driven, very achievement-oriented," perhaps as a carryover from her early need to please her stern father. "I still have so much trouble with my puritan work ethic that if I don't accomplish something every day, I'm a lazy slob and I don't deserve my success," she observes.

At thirty-two, she has already mapped out an ambitious list of things to accomplish in the future. In addition to the film projects she hopes will be generated by her production company, she wants to do more stage work over the years —lots more. "I find it very difficult to think of doing film roles, because I haven't read them yet, but on stage there are many things," she says. "There's a piece I've wanted to do since I was fifteen, Jean Cocteau's *The Human Voice*." The Cocteau play—a one-woman monologue in the form of a telephone conversation—has been performed by both Ingrid Bergman and Liv Ullman. Kathleen feels that, when she is in her midforties, she'll be ready to take it on in her turn.

Will the amazing appeal that Kathleen Turner has radiated from the screen ever since her first slow walk toward Ned Racine in *Body Heat* continue unabated? It's impossible to predict, but it is clear that she is banking on her talent and passion, not on her beauty, to carry her through a long career. "I'd like to keep acting forever," she says. "I don't see why not. There's a very difficult time in a woman's career, sometime in her late thirties or early forties, when she loses that edge of youth and attractiveness and is no longer considered a young leading lady." Then, possibly remembering that she made her film debut at twenty-seven, fully a decade later than Brat Packers like Molly Ringwald or ingenues like Daryl Hannah, she adds, "I don't think I've ever been a *young* leading lady, so I'm not too upset about it. But it's still going to be tough on the ego." She hopes to console herself, however, with roles for mature actresses that will continue to offer the challenge, the "stretch," that is her chief goal in acting: Hedda Gabler and Lady Macbeth, for starters. Such prospects should give even a brilliant and driven performer like Kathleen plenty to shoot for.

She'd like to work harder, produce more, demand more of herself. "I wish there were three of me," she once confessed to a writer for the British magazine *Films and Filming*. "There are so many things I want to do and right now it seems I can only manage about three films a year." Three films with Kathleen's level of involvement and commitment—that's more than some actors would try to do in *three* years. But her intensity is motivated by a desire to explore the limits of her profession, not by a need to rush into roles and rack up a quick string of screen credits. "I don't have to hurry," she says repeatedly, as though trying to convince herself that there will be time to do it all. "I plan to be in this business for a long, long time." Helen Hayes is her inspiration. "Look at her," Kathleen marvels, "doing *Airport*—whatever at the age of 69. I think that's great. I hope to do as well. That's me fifty years from now—*Airport XVII*."

From Nola Aldrich to Matty Walker to Joan Wilder to China Blue, Kathleen has astonished critics and captivated fans with her virtuosity, her style, her almost tangible sensuality, and most of all with her range—her ability to be every woman from the high-school cheerleader to the trampy vamp. It's impossible not to believe that she has many, many more faces still to show. If she does someday appear in *Airport XVII*, it will be worth seeing.

Filmography

1981   *Body Heat*
        Videocassette availability: Warner
        Home Video
        Written by: Lawrence Kasdan
        Directed by: Lawrence Kasdan
        Produced by: Fred T. Gallo/Ladd Com-
        pany
        Distributed by: Warner Brothers
        Starring: Kathleen Turner, William
        Hurt, Richard Crenna, Ted Danson, J.
        A. Preston, Mickey Rourke

1983   *The Man with Two Brains*
        Videocassette availability: Warner
        Home Video
        Written by: Carl Reiner, Steve Martin,
        George Gipe
        Directed by: Carl Reiner
        Produced by: Aspen Film Society/Wil-
        liam E. McEuen/David V. Picker

Distributed by: Warner Brothers
Starring: Steve Martin, Kathleen
Turner, David Warner, Paul Benedict,
Peter Hobbs, Merv Griffin

1984   *A Breed Apart*
Videocassette availability: No
Written by: Paul Wheeler
Directed by: Philippe Mora
Produced by: Hemdale-Sagittarius/
John Daly/Derek Gibson
Starring: Rutger Hauer, Kathleen
Turner, Powers Boothe, Donald Pleas-
ance, Adam Fenwick

Romancing the Stone
Videocassette availability: CBS-Fox
Home Video
Written by: Diane Thomas
Directed by: Robert Zemeckis
Produced by: El Corazon Producciones
S.A./Michael Douglas. Coproducers:
Jack Brodsky, Joel Douglas
Distributed by: Twentieth Century-Fox
Starring: Kathleen Turner, Michael
Douglas, Danny DeVito, Zack Norman,
Manuel Ojeda, Alfonso Arau,
Holland Taylor, Mary Ellen Trainor

Crimes of Passion
Videocassette availability: New World Video
Written by: Barry Sandler
Directed by: Ken Russell
Produced by: Larry Thompson/Donald P. Borchers
Distributed by: New World Pictures
Starring: Kathleen Turner, Anthony Perkins, John Laughlin, Annie Potts

1985   *Prizzi's Honor*
Videocassette availability: Vestron Video
Written by: Richard Condon and Janet Roach
Directed by: John Huston
Produced by: John Foreman
Distributed by: ABC Motion Pictures (now Twentieth Century-Fox)
Starring: Jack Nicholson, Kathleen Turner, Anjelica Huston, William Hickey, Robert Loggia, John Randolph, Lee Richardson, Ann Selepegno, Joseph Ruskin, Michael Lombard, Lawrence Tierney

Jewel of the Nile
Videocassette availability: CBS-Fox Home Video

Written by: Mark Rosenthal and Lawrence Konner
Directed by: Lewis Teague
Produced by: Michael Douglas. Coproducers: Joel Douglas, Jack Brodsky
Distributed by: Twentieth Century-Fox
Starring: Kathleen Turner, Michael Douglas, Danny DeVito, Spiros Focas, Avner Eisenberg, Holland Taylor, Paul David Magid, Howard Jay Patterson, Randall Edwin Nelson, Samuel Ross Williams, Timothy Daniel Furst

1986   *Peggy Sue Got Married*
Videocassette availability: pending
Written by: Jerry Leichtling and Arlene Sarner
Directed by: Francis Coppola
Produced by: Paul R. Gurian/Zoetrope Studios
Distributed by: Tri-Star Pictures
Starring: Kathleen Turner, Nicholas Cage, Kevin O'Connor, Barry Miller, Helen Hunt, Barbara Harris

THE BRIGHTEST STARS...

HOLLYWOOD'S
LEADING LADIES

JULIE CHRISTIE by Michael Feeney Callan
The first biography of the beautiful and enigmatic star. Includes 8 pages of photos.
_____ 90209-3 $3.50 U.S.   _____ 90210-7 $4.50 Can.

AUDREY HEPBURN by Ian Woodward
Fascinating details of this captivating actress are revealed for the first time ever. With 8 pages of enchanting photos.
_____ 90076-7 $3.50 U.S.

MARY TYLER MOORE by Jason Bonderoff
Behind the famous smile of America's sweetheart lies a life of heartbreak, struggle, failure, and ultimate triumph!
_____ 90413-4 $3.95 U.S.   _____ 90414-2 $4.95 Can.

KIM NOVAK: RELUCTANT GODDESS
by Peter Harry Brown
The stunning true story of her superstardom, with 16 pages of fascinating photos.
_____ 90495-9 $3.95 U.S.   _____ 90496-7 $4.95 Can.

JULIE ANDREWS by Robert Windeler
The high and low notes of Hollywood's sweetest voice, including 8 pages of photos.
_____ 90514-9 $3.95 U.S.   _____ 90525-4 $4.95 Can.

ST. MARTIN'S PRESS—MAIL SALES
175 Fifth Avenue, New York, NY 10010

Please send me the book(s) I have checked above. I am enclosing a check or money order (not cash) for $_____ plus 75¢ per order to cover postage and handling (New York residents add applicable sales tax).

Name _____

Address_____

City _____ State_____ Zip Code_____
Allow at least 4 to 6 weeks for delivery